The
Official Rules of
Softball

TRIUMPH

B O O K S
CHICAGO

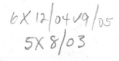

Typographer: Sue Knopf

Front cover photo courtesy of the Amateur Softball Association

Softball Playing Rules copyright by the Amateur Softball Association of America. Revised 1998. Permission to reprint
THE OFFICIAL PLAYING RULES has been granted by
THE AMATEUR SOFTBALL ASSOCIATION OF AMERICA.

This book is available in quantity at special discounts for your group or organization.

For further information, contact:

Triumph Books
644 South Clark Street
Chicago, IL 60605
Tel. (312) 939-3330
Fax (312) 663-3557

User's Guide

This new edition of the Official Rules of Softball as approved by the Amateur Softball Association contains all the current rules governing the playing of the game.

The book is divided into two main sections: the Rules of the Game and Points of Emphasis. The Rules include all official definitions and measurements, pitching regulations for fast pitch, modified pitch, slow pitch, and 16-inch slow pitch, descriptions of the positions, and rules for umpires and protests. The Points of Emphasis includes information on appeals and special playing situations. A third section is an index that cross-references the Rules and the Points of Emphasis. The appendices cover diagrams of the playing field, modifications of the rules for the NAIA, the NCAA, and the NJCAA. There is a detailed Table of Contents to assist you in finding all the rules and information within.

Contents

PART 1
THE OFFICIAL PLAYING RULES

RULE 1: DEFINITIONS 3

RULE 2: THE PLAYING FIELD 17

RULE 3: EQUIPMENT
Section 1. The Official Bat 24
Section 2. Warm-up Bats 26
Section 3. The Official Softball 26
Section 4. Gloves 30
Section 5. Masks, Body Protectors, Shin Guards,
          and Helmets 30
Section 6. Uniform 31
Section 7. All Equipment 34

RULE 4: PLAYERS AND SUBSTITUTES
Section 1. Players 35
Section 2. American Disability Act Rule
          (Slow Pitch Only) 37
Section 3. Designated Player (Fast Pitch Only) 39
Section 4. Extra Player (Slow Pitch Only) 40
Section 5. Re-entry 41
Section 6. Substitutes 42
Section 7. Ejected Player 45
Section 8. Blood Rule 45

RULE 5: THE GAME
Section 1. Home Team 46
Section 2. Fitness of the Ground 46
Section 3. Regulation Game 46
Section 4. Forfeited Games .47
Section 5. Scoring of Runs .48

Contents

Section 6. Game Winner 48
Section 7. Charged Conference 48
Section 8. Home Run Rule
            (Slow Pitch Only) .49
Section 9. Run Ahead Rule
            (Code Article 209F) 51
Section 10. Time Limit Rule
            (Code Article 209G) 51
Section 11. Tie Breaker
            (Code Article 209H) 51
Section 12. Dugout Conduct 52

RULE 6: PITCHING REGULATIONS (Fast Pitch)

Section 1. Preliminaries 53
Section 2. Starting the Pitch .54
Section 3. Legal Delivery 54
Section 4. Intentional Walk .55
Section 5. Defensive Positioning 55
Section 6. Foreign Substance 56
Section 7. Catcher 56
Section 8. Throwing to a Base 57
Section 9. Warm-up Pitches 57
Section 10. No Pitch 58
Section 11. Dropped Ball 58

RULE 6: PITCHING REGULATIONS (Modified Pitch)

Section 1. Preliminaries 59
Section 2. Starting the Pitch .59
Section 3. Legal Delivery 59
Section 4. Intentional Walk .61
Section 5. Defensive Positioning 61
Section 6. Foreign Substance 62
Section 7. Catcher 62
Section 8. Throwing to a Base 62

Section 9. Warm-up Pitches 63
Section 10. No Pitch 64
Section 11. Dropped Ball 64

RULE 6: PITCHING REGULATIONS (Slow Pitch)

Section 1. Preliminaries 65
Section 2. Starting the Pitch .65
Section 3. Legal Delivery 65
Section 4. Defensive Positioning 66
Section 5. Foreign Substance 67
Section 6. Catcher 67
Section 7. Quick Pitch 67
Section 8. Warm-up Pitches .67
Section 9. No Pitch 68

RULE 6: PITCHING REGULATIONS (16 Inch Slow Pitch)

Section 1. Preliminaries 69
Section 2. Starting the Pitch .69
Section 3. Legal Delivery 69
Section 4. Defensive Positioning 71
Section 5. Foreign Substance 71
Section 6. Catcher 72
Section 7. Quick Pitch 72
Section 8. Warm-up Pitches .72
Section 9. No Pitch 73

RULE 7: BATTING

Section 1. On-deck Batter 74
Section 2. Batting Order 74
Section 3. Batting Position 77
Section 4. A Strike Is Called by the Umpire 77
Section 5. A Ball Is Called by the Umpire 79
Section 6. The Batter Is Out .80

RULE 8: **BATTER-RUNNER AND RUNNER**

Section 1. The Batter Becomes a Batter-Runner 82
Section 2. Batter-Runner Is Out 84
Section 3. Touching Bases in Legal Order 87
Section 4. Runners Are Entitled to Advance
            with Liability to Be Put Out 88
Section 5. A Runner Forfeits His Exemption
            from Liability to Be Put Out 89
Section 6. Runners Are Entitled to Advance
            Without Liability to Be Put Out 90
Section 7. A Runner Must Return to His Base 94
Section 8. The Runner Is Out 95
Section 9. Runner Is Not Out 101
Section 10. Running (Senior Men's Only) 103

RULE 9: **PROTESTS** 105

RULE 10: **UMPIRES**

Section 1. Power and Duties .105
Section 2. The Plate Umpire Should 110
Section 3. The Base Umpire Should 110
Section 4. Responsibilities of a Single Umpire 111
Section 5. Change of Umpires 111
Section 6. Umpire's Judgment 111
Section 7. Signals 112
Section 8. Suspension of Play 115
Section 9. Violations and Penalties 116

RULE 11: **SCORING**

Section 1. The Official Scorer Shall Keep
            Records of Each Game 112
Section 2. The Box Score 112
Section 3. A Base Hit 116

Section 4. A Run Batted In .121
Section 5. A Pitcher Shall Be Credited with a Win . .122
Section 6. A Pitcher Shall Be Charged with a Loss . .122
Section 7. The Summary .122
Section 8. A Stolen Base (Fast Pitch Only) 123
Section 9. Records of a Forfeited Game 123
Section 10. Tie Breaker Rule 123

RULE 12: USE OF PLAYING RULES 124

PART 2
POINTS OF EMPHASIS

Appeals 127
Ball Rotation Procedure 130
Bat with Dents 130
Batting with an Illegal Bat 131
Batter Remains in Batter's Box (JO Only) 131
Batting Out of the Batter's Box 132
Catcher's Box 132
Check Swing/Bunt Strike 133
Communication Devices .134
Conferences 134
Delayed Dead Ball 136
Crashing into a Fielder with the Ball 136
Designated Player or DP (Fast Pitch Only) 137
Dugout Conduct 141
Equipment on the Playing Field 141
Extra Player or EP (Slow Pitch Only) 142
Fake Tag 143
Falling Over the Fence on a Catch 144
Hitting the Ball a Second Time 144
Home Runs (Slow Pitch) and Running Bases 145
Imaginary Line or Dead Ball Area 146
Intentionally Dropped Ball 146

Contents

Intentional Walk (Fast Pitch Only) 146
Intentional Walk (Slow Pitch Only) 147
Interference 147
Look-Back Rule (Fast Pitch Only) 150
Media Coverage 152
Obstruction 152
Over-Running First Base 155
Overthrows 155
Pitching (Fast Pitch Only) .156
Pitcher's Uniform 158
Protested Game Upheld and Rescheduled 159
Run Scoring on the Third Out of an Inning 159
Runner Hit by a Fair Ball 160
Shoes 160
Shorthanded Teams 160
Stealing (Slow Pitch) 162
Substitutions 163
Tie Games or Games Called
  Which Are Less Than Regulation 163
Tie Breaker Rule 164

Playing Rules and Points of Emphasis Index 169

Appendix 197

Modifications 202

Softball
Official Rules

Part One
THE OFFICIAL
PLAYING RULES

Wherever "he" or "him" or their related pronouns may appear in this rule book either as words or as parts of words, they have been used for literary purposes and are meant in their generic sense (i.e., to include all humankind, or both male and female sexes).

Where (Fast Pitch Only) is shown, Modified Pitch rules are followed the same as fast pitch with the exception of the pitching rule. Where (Slow Pitch Only) is shown, 16" slow pitch rules are followed the same as slow pitch with the exception of the pitching rule.

The words "Junior Olympic" or the initials "JO" refer to youth softball.

*New rules and/or changes are in **bold letters** in each section.*

Read the "Points of Emphasis" at the end of the rules to clarify various selected rules.

RULE 1 - DEFINITIONS

ALTERED BAT. A bat is considered altered when the physical structure of a legal softball bat has been changed. **A "flare" or "cone" grip attached to the bat handle,** inserting material inside the bat, applying excessive tape (more than two layers) to the bat grip or painting a bat other than at the top or bottom for identification purposes are examples of altering a bat. Replacing the grip with another legal grip is not considered altering a bat. A "flare" or "cone" grip attached to a bat is considered an altered bat.

APPEAL PLAY. An appeal play is a play on which an umpire may not make a decision until requested by a manager, coach or player. The appeal may not be made after any one of the following has occurred:
(1) a legal or illegal pitch,
(2) the pitcher and all infielders have left fair territory,
(3) the umpires have left the field of play.

BASE ON BALLS. A base on balls permits a batter to gain first base without liability to be put out and is awarded to a batter by the umpire when four pitches are judged to be balls. (Slow Pitch Only) If the pitcher desires to walk a batter intentionally, the pitcher may do so by notifying the plate umpire who shall award the batter first base. (Co-Ed Slow Pitch Only) Any walk to a male batter will result in a two base award. With two outs if the male batter receives a base on balls, the female batter has her choice of batting or receiving an automatic walk.

BASE LINE. An imaginary direct line between the bases.

BASE PATH. A direct line between a base and the runner's position at the time a defensive player is attempting (or about to attempt) to tag a runner.

BATTED BALL. A batted ball is any ball that hits the bat or is hit by the bat and lands either in fair or foul territory. No intent to hit the ball is necessary.

BATTER'S BOX. The batter's box is the area in which the batter is positioned while at bat. The lines are considered as being within the batter's box. Prior to the pitch, the batter may touch the lines, but no part of the batter's foot may be outside the lines.

BATTER-RUNNER. A batter-runner is a player who has finished his turn at bat but has not yet been put out or touched first base.

BATTING ORDER. The batting order is the official listing of offensive players by first and last name, in the order in which members of that team must come to bat. NOTE: Uniform number and defensive position must be listed on the lineup sheet.

BLOCKED BALL. A blocked ball is a batted or thrown ball that is touched, stopped or handled by a person not engaged in the game, or which touches any object that is not part of the official equipment or official playing area.

BLOOD RULE. Refers to a player, coach or umpire who is bleeding or who has blood on his uniform and treatment is required.

BUNT. A bunt is a ball that is intentionally tapped with the bat, slowly, within the infield. A bunt should never be considered an infield fly.

CATCH. A catch is a legally caught ball which occurs when the fielder catches a batted, pitched or thrown ball with the hand(s) or glove. In establishing a valid catch, the fielder shall hold the ball long enough to prove complete control of it and/or that the release of the ball is voluntary and intentional. If a player drops the ball after reaching into the glove to remove it or while in the act of throwing, it is a valid catch. If the ball is merely held in the fielder's arm(s) or prevented from dropping to the ground by some part of the fielder's body, equipment or clothing, the catch is not completed until the ball is in the grasp of the fielder's hand(s) or glove. It is not a catch if a fielder, after the fielder touches the ball, collides with another player, umpire or a fence, or falls to the ground and drops the ball as a result of the collision or falling to the ground. A ball which strikes anything other than a defensive player while it is in flight, is ruled the same as if it struck the ground. An illegally caught ball occurs when a fielder catches a batted or thrown ball with anything other than the hand(s) or glove in its proper place. NOTE: Should the catcher catch any fly ball with his mask, the batter is not out.

CATCH AND CARRY. A legal catch that a defensive player carries into dead ball territory. Note: See Rule 8, Section 6J if judged unintentional, or 6K if judged intentional.

CATCHER'S BOX. The area defined by lines which are considered within the catcher's box. The catcher's body and equipment are considered within the box unless touching the ground outside the box. The catcher must remain in the box until:
A. (Fast Pitch Only) The pitch is released.
B. (Slow Pitch Only) The pitched ball is batted, touches the ground or plate or reaches the catcher's box.

CHAMPIONSHIP PLAY. As used in the ASA Softball Playing Rules, the term "Championship Play" shall have the same meaning as is assigned to such term by Article 206 of the ASA Code.

CHARGED CONFERENCE. A charged conference takes place when:
A. **Defensive Conference.** The defensive team requests a suspension of play and a representative enters the

playing field and gives the umpire cause to believe
that a message has been delivered (by any means) to
the pitcher.

B. **Offensive Conference.** The offensive team requests a
suspension of play to allow the manager or other team
representative to confer with the batter and/or
runner(s).

C. **Super Slow Pitch (Defensive). The defensive team
requests a suspension of play, and a representative
enters the playing field and gives the umpire cause to
believe that a message has been delivered (by any
means) to any defensive player.**

CHOPPED BALL. (Slow Pitch Only) A chopped hit ball
occurs when the batter strikes downward with a chop-
ping motion of the bat so that the ball bounces high into
the air.

COACH. A base coach is a member of the team at bat who
takes a place within one of the coach's boxes on the field
to direct the players of the offensive team in running the
bases. Two coaches are allowed. One coach can have in
his possession in the coach's box a score book, pen or
pencil and an indicator, all of which shall be used for
score keeping or record keeping purposes only. No
communication equipment is allowed between the coach,
the dugout, the coach in the other coach's box, or the
spectator areas.

COURTESY RUNNER. (Senior Men's Slow Pitch Only)
A courtesy runner is any player who replaces a runner
without a charged substitution.

CROW HOP. (Fast Pitch Only) A crow hop is defined as the
act of a pitcher who steps, hops or drags off the front of the
pitcher's plate, replants the pivot foot, establishing a second
impetus (or starting point), pushes off from the newly
established starting point and completes the delivery.

DEAD BALL. The term used for a ball that (1) touches any object or player out-of-play, or (2) the umpire has ruled dead. A dead ball line is considered in play.

DEFENSIVE TEAM. The defensive team is the team in the field.

DISLODGED BASE. A dislodged base is a base displaced from its proper position.

DISQUALIFIED PLAYER. Refers to a player who violates the slow pitch home run rule and is disqualified for that game. A substitute can be entered for the disqualified player. If a team is shorthanded, they can continue to play one short. If two players short, the game is forfeited.

DOUBLE PLAY. A double play is a play by the defense in which two offensive players are legally put out as a result of continuous action.

DUGOUT. An out-of-play area designated for players, coaches, bat boys and official representatives of the team only. There shall be no smoking in this area. No communication devices are allowed in this area.

EJECTION. The result of an incident which requires removal from the game by the umpire, whereby the ejected player or coach can no longer participate. A flagrant act will require the player or coach to leave the grounds for the remainder of the game. Any ejected player discovered participating will constitute a forfeit.

FAIR BALL. A batted ball shall be judged according to the relative position of the ball and the foul line, including the foul pole, and not as to whether the fielder is on fair or foul territory at the time the fielder touches the ball. It does not matter whether the ball first touches fair or foul territory, as long as it does not touch anything foreign to the natural ground in foul territory and complies with all other aspects of a fair ball. A fair ball is a legally batted ball that:

A. Settles or is touched on or over fair territory between home and first base or between home and third base.

B. Bounds over or past first or third base which is in fair territory, regardless of where the ball hits after going over the base.

C. While on or over fair territory, touches the person, attached equipment or clothing of a player or an umpire.

D. **While over fair territory, a runner interferes with a defensive player attempting to field a batted ball.**

E. Touches first, second or third base.

F. First falls or is first touched on or over fair territory beyond first, second or third base.

G. While over fair territory, passes out of the playing field beyond the outfield fence.

H. Hits the foul pole.

FAIR TERRITORY. Fair territory is that part of the playing field within, and including, the first and third base foul lines from home plate to the bottom of the playing field fence and perpendicularly upwards.

FAKE TAG. A form of obstruction by a fielder who neither has the ball nor is about to receive the ball, and which impedes the progress of a runner either advancing or returning to a base. The runner does not have to stop or slide. Merely slowing down when a fake tag is attempted would constitute obstruction.

FIELDER. A fielder is any player of the team in the field.

FLY BALL. A fly ball is any ball batted into the air.

FORCE OUT. A force out is an out which may be made only when a runner loses the right to the base that the runner is occupying because the batter becomes a batter-runner, and before the batter-runner or a succeeding runner has been put out. NOTE: If the forced runner, after touching the next base, retreats for any reason towards the base last occupied, the force play is reinstated and the runner may again be put out if the defense tags the runner or the base to which the runner is forced.

FOUL BALL. A foul ball is a batted ball that:
A. Settles or is touched on or over foul territory between home and first base or between home and third base.
B. Bounds or rolls past first or third base on or over foul territory.
C. While over foul territory, touches the person, attached equipment or clothing of a player or an umpire, or any object foreign to the natural ground.
D. While over foul territory, a runner interferes with a defensive player attempting to field a batted ball.
E. First hits the ground or is first touched over foul territory beyond first or third base. A caught fly ball is not a foul ball.
F. Touches the batter or the bat in the batter's hand(s) a second time while the batter is within the batter's box.

FOUL TIP. A batted ball which goes directly from the bat, not higher than the batter's head, to the catcher's hand(s) or glove and is legally caught by the catcher. NOTE: Any batted ball that goes directly from the bat, not higher than the batter's head to any part of the catcher's body or equipment other than the hand(s) or glove is a foul ball and dead.

HELMET.
A. **Offensive:** All helmets must have double ear flaps and be approved by the National Operating Committee on Standards for Athletic Equipment (NOCSAE).
B. **Defensive:** Any player may wear an approved helmet with or without earflaps. It must have a bill.
C. **Catcher:** These helmets currently do not have NOCSAE standards but must be worn where required.

HOME TEAM. The home team shall be designated by mutual agreement or by a flip of a coin, unless otherwise stated in the rules of the organization which the schedule of games is being played.

ILLEGAL BAT. An illegal bat is one that does not meet the requirements of Rule 3, Section 1. (For Illegal Warm-Up Bat, see Rule 3, Section 2)

ILLEGALLY BATTED BALL. An illegally batted ball occurs when the batter hits the ball fair or foul and:
   A. When, at the time the bat makes contact with the ball, the entire foot is completely outside the lines of the batter's box and on the ground.
   B. When, at the time the bat makes contact with the ball, any part of the foot is touching home plate.
   C. An illegal or altered bat is used.

ILLEGAL BATTER (Fast Pitch Only). A defensive only player (DEFO) who bats for any offensive player other than the DP. The player is ejected.

ILLEGAL PITCHER. A player legally in the game, but one who may not pitch as a result of being removed from the pitching position by the umpire because of:
   A. Two charged defensive conferences in one inning.
   B. (Slow Pitch Only) Pitching with excessive speed after a warning.
   C. (Slow Pitch Only) After a warning, making any motion to deliver a pitch prior to having one or both feet in contact with the pitching plate.
   EFFECT: If an illegal pitcher returns to the pitching position and has thrown one pitch the illegal player is ejected from the game.

ILLEGAL RE-ENTRY. An illegal re-entry occurs when:
   A. A starting player returns to the game a second time after twice being substituted.
   B. A starting player returns to the game but is not in his original position in the offensive lineup.

C. A legal substitute returns to the game after being replaced.

ILLEGAL RUNNER. Placing an offensive player already in the lineup who runs for another offensive player, or the DEFO running for a player other than the DP. The illegal player is ejected. EXCEPTION: Senior Men's Slow Pitch.

ILLEGAL SUBSTITUTE. A player who has entered the game without reporting.

IN FLIGHT. In flight is the term used for any batted, thrown or pitched ball which has not yet touched the ground or some object or person other than a fielder.

IN JEOPARDY. In jeopardy is a term indicating that the ball is in play and an offensive player may be put out.

INELIGIBLE PLAYER. A player who does not meet the requirements of ASA Code. The determination of eligibility is not the responsibility of the umpire. The use of an ineligible player will constitute a forfeit if properly protested.

INFIELD. The infield is that portion of the field in fair territory which includes areas normally covered by infielders.

INFIELD FLY. A fair fly ball (not including a line drive or an attempted bunt) which can be caught by an infielder with ordinary effort when first and second bases or first, second and third bases are occupied before two are out. Any defensive player who takes a position in the infield at the start of the pitch shall be considered an infielder for the purpose of this rule. The infield fly is ruled when the ball reaches the highest point based on the position of the closest infielder regardless who makes the play. When it seems apparent that a batted ball will be an infield fly, the umpire shall immediately declare: "Infield

Fly." The ball is alive and runners may advance at the risk of the ball being caught. The runner can tag up and advance once the batted ball is touched (prior to catching), the same as on any fly ball. If a declared infield fly becomes a foul ball, it is treated the same as any foul.

INNING. An inning is that portion of a game within which the teams alternate on offense and defense and in which there are three outs for each team. A new inning begins immediately after the final out of the previous inning.

INTERFERENCE. Interference is the act of an offensive player or team member, umpire, or spectator which impedes, hinders, or confuses a defensive player attempting to execute a play.

JUNIOR OLYMPIC PLAYER. Any player 18 years and under who has not reached their 19th birthday prior to September 1.
NOTE: If Junior Olympic players play on an adult team, it is considered playing in an adult league and adult rules will be in effect.

LEAPING. (Fast Pitch Only) An act by the pitcher which causes the pitcher to be airborne on the initial move and push from the pitcher's plate. The momentum built by the forward movement of the pitcher causes the entire body including both the pivot foot and the non-pivot foot to be in the air and moving toward home plate as the delivery is completed. With this style of pitching, the pitcher will release the ball prior to or simultaneously with the return to the ground. The pivot foot will then slide to the side and drag as the pitcher follows through or completes the delivery. This follow through should not be confused with replanting and gaining a second starting point (defined as the "crow hop"), but simply a finish or follow through of the leap style of pitching. At the completion of the leap, the non pivot foot is planted but will not allow the pitcher to gain further distance towards the plate, therefore the slide and drag of the pivot foot is a legal act.

LEGAL TAG. A legal tag occurs when a runner or batter-runner who is not touching a base is tagged by the ball while it is securely held in a fielder's hand(s) or glove. The ball is not considered as having been securely held if it is juggled or dropped by the fielder after having tagged the runner, unless the runner deliberately knocks the ball from the hand(s) of the fielder.

LINE DRIVE. A fly ball that is batted sharply and directly into the playing field. NOTE: A line drive should never be considered an infield fly.

OBSTRUCTION. Obstruction is the act of:
   A. A defensive player or team member which hinders or prevents a batter from striking at or hitting a pitched ball.
   B. A fielder, who is not (1) in possession of the ball, (2) in the act of fielding a batted ball, or (3) about to receive a thrown ball, which impedes the progress of a runner or batter-runner who is legally running bases.

OFFENSIVE TEAM. The offensive team is the team at bat.

ON-DECK BATTER. The on-deck batter is the offensive player whose name follows the name of the batter in the batting order.

OUTFIELD. The outfield is that portion of the field in fair territory which is not normally covered by an infielder.

OVERSLIDE. An overslide is the act of an offensive player when, as a runner, overslides a base the player is attempting to reach. It is usually caused when the player's momentum causes the player to lose contact with the base which then causes the player to be in jeopardy. The batter-runner may overslide first base without being in jeopardy.

OVERTHROW. An overthrow occurs when a thrown ball from a fielder goes beyond the boundary lines of the playing field (dead ball territory) or becomes a blocked ball.

PASSED BALL. (Fast Pitch Only) A passed ball is a legally delivered ball that should have been held or controlled by the catcher with ordinary effort.

PIVOT FOOT. (Fast Pitch Only) The pivot foot is that foot which must remain in contact with the pitcher's plate prior to the pitch and pushes off the pitcher's plate. (Slow Pitch Only) The pivot foot is the foot which the pitcher must keep in constant contact with the pitcher's plate until the ball is released.

PLAY BALL. Play ball is the term used by the plate umpire to indicate that play shall start and shall not be declared until all defensive players are in fair territory except the catcher, who must be in the catcher's box.

PROTESTS. There are three types of protests:
- A. Misinterpretation of a playing rule—must be made before the next pitch or, if on the last play of the game, before the umpires leave the playing field.
- B. Illegal substitute or re-entry—must be made while they are in the game and before the umpires leave the playing field.
- C. Ineligible player—can be made any time during or after the game. Eligibility is the decision of the protest committee.

QUICK RETURN PITCH. A pitch made by the pitcher with the obvious attempt to catch the batter off balance. This would be before the batter takes a desired position in the batter's box or while the batter is still off balance as a result of the previous pitch.

RUNNER. A runner is an offensive player who has reached first base and has not yet been put out.

SACRIFICE FLY. A sacrifice fly is scored when, with fewer than two outs, the batter scores a runner with a fly ball or line drive that is:
  A. Caught.
  B. Dropped by an outfielder (or an infielder running into the outfield), and, in the scorer's judgment, the runner could have scored after the catch had the fly ball or line drive been caught.

STARTING PLAYER. A starting player shall be official when the lineup sheet is inspected and approved by the plate umpire and team manager at the pre-game meeting. The names may be entered on the official score sheet in advance of this meeting; however, changes can be made at the pre-game meeting with no charged substitutions.

STEALING. (Fast Pitch Only) Stealing is the act of a runner attempting to advance during a pitch to the batter. (Super Slow Pitch Only) Runners can advance once the pitched ball reaches home plate.

STRIKE ZONE. When a batter assumes a natural batting stance adjacent to home plate, the strike zone is that space over any part of home plate between the batter's:
  A. (Fast Pitch Only) Arm pits and the top of the knees.
  B. (Slow Pitch Only) Back shoulder and the front knee.

SUBSTITUTE. Any member of a team's roster who is not listed as a starting player, or a starting player who re-enters the game.

TRAPPED BALL. A trapped ball is:
  A. A batted fly ball or line drive which hits the ground or a fence prior to being caught,
  B. A thrown ball to any base for a force out which is caught with the glove over the ball on the ground rather than under the ball, and/or
  C. (Fast Pitch Only) A pitched ball which touches the ground on a strike prior to the catcher catching it.

TIME. Time is the term used by the umpire to order the suspension of play.

TRIPLE PLAY. A triple play is a continuous action play by the defense in which three offensive players are legally put out as a result of a continuous action.

TURN AT BAT. A turn at bat begins when a player first enters the batter's box and continues until the player is put out, becomes a batter-runner or is substituted for while at bat. NOTE: A runner that is ruled out on a fair batted ball or caught fly ball for the third out will still count as a turn at bat.

WILD PITCH. (Fast Pitch Only) A wild pitch is a legally delivered ball that the catcher cannot catch or stop and control with ordinary effort.

RULE 2 - THE PLAYING FIELD

SECTION 1. The playing field is the area within which the ball may be legally played and fielded. There shall be a clear and unobstructed area between the foul lines and within the radius of the prescribed fence distances from home plate.

NOTE: If the base distances or the pitching distance is found to be at the wrong dimensions during the course of the game, correct the error, with no penalty, and continue playing the game. Every effort should be made by the umpire to obtain the correct dimensions.

SECTION 2. Ground or special rules establishing the limits of the playing field may be agreed upon by leagues or opposing teams. Any obstruction on fair ground less than the prescribed fence distances from home plate should be clearly marked for the umpire's information. If using a baseball field, the mound should be removed and the backstop distance must meet those prescribed (minimum of 25 feet [7.62m] or a maximum of 30 feet [9.14m] from home plate).

SECTION 3. For the layout of the diamond, refer to drawing showing official dimensions for a softball diamond. This section serves as an example for laying out a diamond with 60-foot bases and a 46-foot pitching distance.

To determine the position of home plate, draw a line in the direction desired to lay the diamond. Drive a stake at the corner of home plate nearest the catcher. Fasten a cord to this stake and tie knots, or otherwise mark the cord, at 46 feet (14.02m), 60 feet (18.29m), 84 feet 10¼ inches (25.86m), and at 120 feet (36.58m). Place the cord (without stretching) along the direction line and place a stake at the 46-foot (14.02m) marker. This will be the front line at

OFFICIAL DISTANCE TABLE (ADULT)

ADULT	DIVISION	BASES	PITCHING	MIN. FENCE	MAX. FENCE
Fast Pitch	Women	60' (18.29 m)	40' (12.19 m)	200' (60.96 m)	250' (76.20 m)
	Men	60' (18.29 m)	46' (14.02 m)	225' (68.58 m)	250' (76.20 m)
	Jr. Men	60' (18.29 m)	46' (14.02 m)	225' (68.58 m)	250' (76.20 m)
Modified Pitch	Women	60' (18.29 m)	40' (12.19 m)	200' (60.96 m)	
	Men	60' (18.29 m)	46' (14.02 m)	265' (80.80 m)	
Slow Pitch	Women	65' (19.81 m)	50' (15.24 m)	265' (80.80 m)	275' (83.82 m)
	Men	65' (19.81 m)	50' (15.24 m)	275' (83.82 m)	315' (96.01 m)
	Coed	65' (19.81 m)	50' (15.24 m)	275' (83.82 m)	300' (91.44 m)
	Super	70' (20.73 m)	50' (15.24 m)	325' (99.08 m)	
16-Inch Pitch	Women	55' (16.76 m)	38' (11.58 m)	200' (60.96 m)	
	Men	55' (16.76 m)	38' (11.58 m)	250' (76.20 m)	

the middle of the pitcher's plate. Along the same line, drive a stake at the 84-foot 10¼-inch (25.68m) marker. This will be the center of second base. Place the 120-foot (36.58m) marker at the center of second base and, taking hold of the cord at the 60-foot (18.29m) marker, walk to the right of the direction line until the cord is taut and drive a stake at the 60-foot (18.29m) marker. This will be the outside corner of first base and the cord will now form the lines to first and second bases. Again, holding the cord at the 60-foot (18.29m) marker, walk across the field and, in like manner, mark the outside corner of third base. Home plate, first base and third base are wholly inside the diamond. To check the diamond, place the home plate end of the cord at the first base stake and the 120-foot (36.58m) marker at third base. The 60-foot (18.29m) marker should now check at home plate and the middle of second base.

In the layout of a 65-foot base path diamond, follow the same procedure with the following substitute dimensions: 65 foot (19.81m), 130 foot (39.62m), and 91 feet 11 inches (28.07m). Check all distances with a steel tape whenever possible.

A. The three-foot (0.91m) line is drawn parallel to and three feet (0.91m) from the baseline, starting at a point halfway between home plate and first base.

B. The batter's on-deck circle is a five-foot (1.52m) circle (2½-foot [0.76m] radius) placed adjacent to the end of the players' bench or dugout area closest to home plate.

C. The batter's box, one on each side of home plate shall measure three feet (0.91m) by seven feet (2.13m). The inside lines of the batter's box shall be six inches (15.24cm) from home plate. The front line of the box shall be four feet (1.22m) in front of a line drawn through the center of home plate. The lines are con-

OFFICIAL DISTANCE TABLE (YOUTH)

YOUTH	DIVISION	BASES	PITCHING	MIN. FENCE	MAX. FENCE
Fast Pitch	G10-U	55' (16.76 m)	35' (10.67 m)	150' (45.72 m)	175' (53.34 m)
	G12-U	60' (18.29 m)	35' (10.67 m)	175' (53.34 m)	200' (60.96 m)
	G14-U	60' (18.29 m)	40' (12.19 m)	175' (53.34 m)	200' (60.96 m)
	G16-U	60' (18.29 m)	40' (12.19 m)	200' (60.96 m)	225' (68.58 m)
	G18-U	60' (18.29 m)	40' (12.19 m)	200' (60.96 m)	225' (68.58 m)
	B10-U	55' (16.76 m)	35' (10.67 m)	150' (45.72 m)	175' (53.34 m)
	B12-U	60' (18.29 m)	40' (12.19 m)	175' (53.34 m)	200' (60.96 m)
	B14-U	60' (18.29 m)	46' (14.02 m)	175' (53.34 m)	200' (60.96 m)
	B16-U	60' (18.29 m)	46' (14.02 m)	200' (60.96 m)	225' (68.58 m)
	B18-U	60' (18.29 m)	46' (14.02 m)	200' (60.96 m)	225' (68.58 m)
Slow Pitch	G10-U	55' (16.76 m)	35' (10.67 m)	150' (45.72 m)	175' (53.34 m)
	G12-U	60' (18.29 m)	40' (12.19 m)	175' (53.34 m)	200' (60.96 m)
	G14-U	65' (19.81 m)	50' (15.24 m)	225' (68.58 m)	250' (76.20 m)
	G16-U	65' (19.81 m)	50' (15.24 m)	225' (68.58 m)	250' (76.20 m)
	G18-U	65' (19.81 m)	50' (15.24 m)	225' (68.58 m)	250' (76.20 m)
	B10-U	55' (16.76 m)	35' (10.67 m)	150' (45.72 m)	175' (53.34 m)
	B12-U	60' (18.29 m)	40' (12.19 m)	175' (53.34 m)	200' (60.96 m)
	B14-U	65' (19.81 m)	50' (15.24 m)	250' (76.20 m)	275' (83.82 m)
	B16-U	65' (19.81 m)	50' (15.24 m)	275' (83.82 m)	300' (91.44 m)
	B18-U	65' (19.81 m)	50' (15.24 m)	275' (83.82 m)	300' (91.44 m)

sidered as being within the batter's box.

D. The catcher's box shall be 10 feet (3.05m) in length from the rear outside corners of the batters' boxes and shall be eight feet, five inches (2.57m) wide.

E. Each coach's box is behind a line 15 feet (4.57m) long drawn outside the diamond. The line is parallel to and eight feet (2.44m) from the first and third base line, extended from the bases toward home plate.

F. The pitcher's plate shall be of rubber or wood, 24 inches (60.96cm) long and six inches (15.24cm) wide. The top of the plate shall be level with the ground. The front of the plate shall be the prescribed pitching distances from the back point of the plate. It shall be permanently attached to the ground at distances indicated in Rule 2, Section 1. (Fast Pitch Only) There shall be a 16-foot (4.88m) circle, eight feet (2.44m) in radius, drawn from the center of the pitcher's plate. The lines drawn around the pitcher's plate are considered inside the circle.

G. Home plate shall be made of rubber or other suitable material. It shall be a five-sided figure, 17 inches (43.18cm) wide across the edge facing the pitcher's plate. The sides shall be parallel to the inside lines of the batter's box and shall be 8½ inches (21.59cm) long. The sides of the point facing the catcher shall be 12 inches (30.48cm) long.

    1. (Senior Men's Slow Pitch) The second home plate shall be placed eight feet from the back tip of home plate on an extended line from first base. A line shall be drawn from third base to the second home plate. (See diagram.)

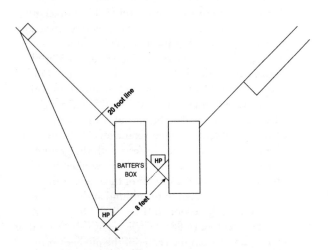

H. The bases, other than home plate, shall be 15 inches (38.10cm) square, shall be made of canvas or other suitable material and not more than five inches (12.70cm) in thickness. The bases should be properly fastened in position.

  1. The double base is approved for use at first base. This base is 15 by 30 inches and made of canvas or other suitable material. Half the base is white (over fair territory) and half is orange or green (over foul territory). It should not be more than five inches (12.70cm) in thickness. NOTE: When using the double base at first, the following rules should be enforced:

    a. A batted ball hitting the white portion is declared fair and a batted ball hitting the colored portion is declared foul.

b. Whenever a play is being made on the batter-runner, the defense must use the white portion and the batter-runner the colored portion. On extra base hits or balls hit to the outfield when there is no play being made at the double base, the batter-runner may touch the white or colored portion. Should the batter-runner return, the runner must return to the white portion. NOTE: The batter-runner is out when there is a play being made at first base and the batter-runner touches only the white portion, providing the defense appeals prior to the batter-runner returning to first base.

c. **On any force out attempt from the foul side of first base, the H-1-(c) defense and the batter-runner can use either the orange or white portion. NOTE: This includes overthrows.**

d. When tagging up on a fly ball, the white portion must be used.

e. (Fast Pitch & 16-Inch Slow Pitch Only) On an attempted pick-off play, the runner must return to the white portion.

2. (Senior Men's Slow Pitch) The double first base shall be used in this division of play.

RULE 3 - EQUIPMENT

SECTION 1. THE OFFICIAL BAT.

A. Shall be made of one piece of hardwood, or formed from a block of wood consisting of two or more pieces of wood bonded together with an adhesive in such a way that the grain direction of all pieces is essentially parallel to the length of the bat.

B. Shall be metal, plastic, graphite, carbon, magnesium, fiberglass, ceramic or any other composite material approved by the ASA. Any new composite construction bat must be reviewed and approved by the ASA. NOTE: Bats made of or containing TIMETAL 15-3 or TELEDYNE 15-333 titanium alloy shall not be used until further testing is completed.

C. May be laminated but must contain only wood or adhesive and have a clear finish (if finished).

D. Shall be round or three-sided and shall be smooth. If the barrel end has a knurled finish the maximum surface roughness is no more than 250 if measured by a profilometer or 4/1000 if measured by a spectrograph.

E. Shall not be more than 34 inches (87.0cm) long, nor exceed 38 ounces (1100.0g) in weight.

F. If round, shall not be more than 2¼ inches (6.0cm) in diameter at its largest part; and if three-sided, shall not exceed 2¼ inches (6.0cm) on the hitting surface. A tolerance of ½₂ inch (0.90mm) is permitted to allow for expansion on the round bat.
NOTE: If the bat ring goes over the bat it should be considered a legal bat.

G. If metal, may be angular.

H. Shall not have exposed rivets, pins, rough or sharp edges or any form of exterior fastener that would present a hazard. A metal bat shall be free of burrs or cracks.

I. If metal, shall not have a wooden handle.

J. Shall have a safety grip of cork, tape (no smooth,

plastic tape) or composition material. The safety grip shall not be less than 10 inches (25.0cm) long and shall not extend more than 15 inches (40.0cm) from the small end of the bat. Any molded finger-formed grip made by the bat manufacturer, if used, must be permanently attached to the bat or attached to the bat with safety tape and must be approved by the Equipment Standards Committee. Resin, pine tar or spray substances placed on the safety grip to enhance the grip are permissible on the grip only. Tape applied to any bat must be continuously spiral. It does not have to be a solid layer of tape. It may not exceed two layers. Taping of a bat less than the required length is considered illegal. APPROVED GRIPS: Bear Grip, Rotary Grip, Dome Style Power Grip, Finger Style and Sure Grip are all approved.

K. If metal, and not made of one-piece construction with the barrel end closed, shall have a rubber or vinyl plastic or other approved material insert firmly secured at the large end of the bat.

L. Shall have a safety knob of a minimum of ¼ inch protruding at a 90-degree angle from the handle. It may be molded, lathed, welded or permanently fastened. A "flare" or "cone" grip attached to the bat will be considered altered. The knob may be taped as long as there is no violation of this section.

M. Shall be marked OFFICIAL SOFTBALL by the manufacturer. If the words OFFICIAL SOFTBALL cannot be read due to wear and tear on the bat, the bat should be declared legal if it is legal in all other aspects.
NOTE: Softball bats used in ASA championship tournament play must be approved by the Equipment Standards Committee. Manufacturers must submit all new designed bats to the ASA Equipment Standards Committee for approval prior to sales.

N. Beginning January 1, 2000, only bats which bear an ASA approved certification mark signifying compliance with the ASA bat performance standards then in effect will be allowed for use in ASA Championship Play.

SECTION 2. WARM-UP BATS.

The warm-up bat should meet the following requirements to be approved:

A. Stamped with ¼ inch letters WB on either end of the bat or marked in one-inch letters the words WARM-UP BAT only on the barrel end of the bat.

B. Shall have a safety grip of at least 10 inches (25.0cm) and no more than 15 inches (40.0cm) extended from the knob.

C. Be of one-piece construction or a one-piece permanently assembled bat which clearly distinguishes itself as a warm-up bat and is approved by the Equipment Standards Committee.

D. Shall have a safety knob of a minimum of ¼ inch protruding at a 90 degree angle from the handle. It may be molded, lathed, welded or permanently fastened.

E. No attachments (i.e. donuts, fans, etc.) are allowed on an official bat except the Pow'R Wrap warm-up attachment. (Rule 7, Section 1C).

WARM-UP BATS APPROVED

All-Star, Bratt's Bat, Dirx dX250 (Dirx Company), Dudley, Hillerich & Bradsby (Louisville Slugger), Whip-O, Mega bat, Sledge Hammer (Steele's Sports), Swingmaster (J. deBeer), TopHand (Switch-Hitter, Inc.), Worth and Stombaugh.

SECTION 3. THE OFFICIAL SOFTBALL.

A. Shall be a regular, smooth-seamed, flat-surfaced, pebble-textured (Slow Pitch Only) or dimple-textured ball with concealed stitches.

B. Shall have a center core made of either No. 1 quality long fiber kapok, a mixture of cork and rubber, a polyurethane mixture or other materials approved by the ASA.

C. May be hand or machine-wound with a fine quality twisted yarn and covered with latex or rubber cement.

D. Shall have a cover cemented to the ball by application of cement to the underside of the cover and sewn with waxed thread of cotton or linen. If the cover is molded, it may be bonded to the core or be of the same composition as the core. Either molded type must have an authentic facsimile of stitching as approved by the ASA.

E. Shall have a cover of chrome-tanned, top-grain horse-hide or cowhide, synthetic material or other materials approved by the ASA.

F. The 12-inch (30.0cm) ball shall be between 11⅞ inches (30.0cm) and 12⅛ inches (31.0cm) in circumference and shall weigh between 6¼ ounces (180.0g) and seven ounces (200.0g). The smooth-seamed style shall not have fewer than 88 stitches in each cover, sewn by the two-needle method, or with an authentic facsimile of stitching as approved by the ASA.

G. The 11-inch (27.0cm) ball shall be between 10⅞ inches (27.0cm) and 11⅛ inches (28.0cm) in circumference. It shall weigh between 5⅞ ounces (165.0g) and 6⅛ ounces (175.0g). The smooth-seamed style shall not have fewer than 80 stitches in each cover, sewn by the two-needle method, or with an authentic facsimile of stitching as approved by the ASA.

H. The white-stitch 12-inch ball with a COR of .50 or under shall be used in the following ASA play: men's and women's fast pitch, boys and girls 12-, 14-, 16-, and 18-under fast pitch, and boys 14-, 16-, and 18-under slow pitch. It must be marked ASA 5095.

OFFICIAL SOFTBALL MEASUREMENTS

SOFTBALL	THREAD COLOR	MIN. SIZE	MAX. SIZE	MIN. WEIGHT	MAX. WEIGHT	MARKING
11" SP (27.0 cm)	red	10⅞ in 27.0cm	11⅛ in 28.0cm	5⅞ oz 165.0g	6⅛ oz 175.0g	ASA-4795 ASA Logo
11" FP (27.0 cm)	white	10⅞ in 27.0cm	11⅛ in 28.0cm	5⅞ oz 165.0g	6⅛ oz 175.0g	ASA-5095 ASA Logo
12" FP (30.0cm)	white	11⅞ in. 30.0cm	12⅛ in. 31.0cm	6¼ oz 180.0g	7 oz 200.0g	ASA-5095 ASA Logo
12" SP (30.0cm)	red	11⅞ in. 30.0cm	12⅛ in. 31.0cm	6¼ oz 180.0g	7 oz 200.0g	ASA-4795 ASA Logo
12" SP (30.0cm)	gold	11⅞ in. 30.0cm	12⅛ in. 31.0cm	6¼ oz 180.0g	7 oz 200.0g	ASA-4795 ASA Logo
16" SP (41.0cm)	white	15⅞ in. 40.9cm	16⅛ in. 41.0cm	9 oz 225.0g	10 oz 283.0g	ASA Logo

I. The white-stitch 11-inch ball with a COR of .50 or under shall be used in the following ASA play: boys and girls 10-under fast pitch. It must be marked ASA 5095.

J. The red-stitch (and/or red indelible stamping as approved by the ASA) 12-inch ball with a COR of .47 and under shall be used in the following ASA play: men's slow pitch and coed (male batters only) slow pitch **and all modified pitch**. It must be marked ASA 4795. NOTE: The .50 COR yellow optic, red-stitch ball is not legal for slow pitch **or modified pitch** play.

K. The red-stitch (and/or red indelible stamping as approved by the ASA) 11-inch ball with a COR of .47 and under shall be used in the following ASA play: women's slow pitch, coed slow pitch (women batters only), boys 10- and 12-under slow pitch and girls 12-, 14-, 16-, and 18-under slow pitch. It must be marked ASA 4795.

EFFECT - J-K: If the wrong ball is used in coed play, the manager of the offensive team has the option of taking the result of the play or having the last batter rebat and assume the ball and strike count prior to the wrong ball being discovered.

L. The gold stitch 12-inch ball with a COR of .44 and under shall be used in the super slow pitch division when fences are less than 325 feet. It must be marked ASA 4495.

M. Softballs used in ASA play must meet standards set by the ASA as shown on the chart and must be stamped with the ASA logo.

N. **Beginning January 1, 1999, for all balls used in ASA Championship Play, the load force required to compress the ball 0.25 inches must not exceed 750 pounds when such balls are tested in accordance with the ASTM test method for measuring compres-**

sion-displacement of softballs. Rule effective for 1999.

SECTION 4. **GLOVES** may be worn by any player, but mitts may be used only by the catcher and first baseman. No top lacing, webbing or other device between the thumb and body of the glove or mitt worn by a first baseman or catcher, or a glove worn by any fielder; shall be more than five inches (12.70cm) in length. (Fast Pitch Only) The pitcher's glove shall not be partially or one solid color of white or gray.

SECTION 5. MASKS, BODY PROTECTORS, SHIN GUARDS AND HELMETS.

A. (Fast Pitch Only) Adult catchers must wear masks with throat protectors. An extended wire protector may be worn in lieu of an attached throat protector.

B. (Slow Pitch Only) Junior Olympic catchers must wear an approved batter's helmet with ear flaps, or the catcher's helmet and mask. The throat protector is optional on the catcher's mask.

C. (Fast Pitch Only) Junior Olympic catchers must wear a mask with throat protector, approved helmet with ear flaps, shin guards which offer protection to the knee caps and body protector. An extended wire protector may be worn in lieu of an attached throat protector.

NOTE: Any player warming up a Junior Olympic pitcher must wear a mask with throat protector and approved helmet with ear flaps.

NOTE: (Sections A-B-C) The hockey style face mask is approved for usage by catchers.

D. **HELMETS.**

1. **OFFENSE.** All adult fast pitch, modified pitch and all Junior Olympic offensive players,

including the on-deck batter and Junior Olympic players acting as coaches in the coach's box, must properly wear double ear flap NOC-SAE-approved batting helmets. Any offensive player may wear an approved helmet of similar color as the team caps. Batting helmets that are broken, cracked, dented, or that have been illegally altered are prohibited from use.

EFFECT: Failure to wear the batting helmet when ordered to do so by the umpire shall cause the player to be ejected from the game. Wearing the helmet improperly or removing the helmet during a live ball play and judged by the umpire to be a deliberate act shall cause the violator to be declared out immediately. The ball remains alive.

NOTE: Calling a runner out for removing a helmet does not remove force play situations. Umpires should use discretion as to the intent of the rule concerning player safety.

2. **DEFENSE.** Any defensive player may wear an approved helmet of similar color as the team caps.

E. **FACE MASKS. An approved plastic face mask/guard can be worn by any defensive (other than catcher) or offensive player. Face masks/guards that are cracked or deformed, or if padding has deteriorated or is missing is prohibited from use. Approved is the SportsGuard face mask.**

SECTION 6. UNIFORM.

All players on a team shall properly wear uniforms that are alike in color, trim and style. If because of the blood rule a change is required and the uniform part does not match, the player will not be penalized. Coaches must be neatly attired and dressed alike or in team uniform and in accordance with the color code of the team. All protective equipment should be worn properly.

NOTE: If a player is requested by the umpire to remove jewelry, illegal shoes or illegal parts of the uniform and they refuse, the player will not be allowed to play.

A. **HEADWEAR.**
    1. (Fast Pitch Male) Ball caps are mandatory, must be alike and worn properly.
    2. (Female Fast Pitch & All Slow Pitch) Ball caps, visors and headbands are optional for players. If worn, they can be mixed, but must be worn properly. If one type or more than one type is worn, they all must be of the same color. Handkerchiefs and visors cannot be worn around the head or neck.
       NOTE: Plastic visors are not allowed.
    3. If a coach wears headwear, it must be approved.

B. **PANTS/SLIDING PANTS.** All players' pants shall be either all long or all short in style, or may be mixed (long and short) as long as they are alike in color. Players may wear a solid-colored pair of sliding pants. It is not mandatory that all players wear sliding pants, but if more than one player wears them, they must be alike in color and style. No player may wear ragged, frayed or slit legs on exposed sliding pants.

C. **UNDERSHIRTS.** Players may wear a solid-colored undershirt (it may be white). It is not mandatory that all players wear an undershirt, but if more than one player wears one, they must be alike. No player may wear ragged, frayed or slit sleeves on exposed undershirts.

D. **NUMBERS.** An Arabic number of contrasting color at least six inches (15.24cm) high must be worn on the back of all uniform shirts. No players on the same team may wear identical numbers. (Numbers 3 and 03 are examples of identical numbers.) Players without numbers will not be permitted to play. If duplicate numbers exist, only one of the players may play at a time. There is no penalty for a player wearing a wrong number. Correct the number in the scorebook and continue play.

NOTE: There is no penalty for duplicate numbers. Just ask one player to change jerseys, or require a substitute to enter for one of the players.

E. **CASTS/PROSTHESES.** All casts and splints must be padded. Prostheses may be worn. Braces with exposed hard surfaces must be padded. Any of this equipment judged by the umpire to be potentially dangerous is illegal. NOTE: Any decision by the umpire should be based on whether or not a device worn or used by an individual with a disability changes the fundamental nature of the game or poses a significant risk to the safety of other players.

F. **JEWELRY.** Exposed jewelry, which is judged by the umpire to be dangerous, must be removed and may not be worn during the game.

NOTE: Medical alert bracelets or necklaces are not considered jewelry. If worn, they must be taped to the body so the medical alert information remains visible.

G. **SHOES.** Must be worn by all players. A shoe shall be considered official if it is made with either canvas or leather uppers or similar material(s). The soles may be either smooth or have soft or hard rubber cleats. Ordinary metal sole or heel plates may be used if the spikes on the plates do not extend more than ¾ of an inch (1.91cm) from the sole or heel of the shoe. Shoes with round metal spikes are illegal. No shoes with detachable cleats that screw ON are allowed; however,

shoes with detachable cleats that screw INTO the shoe
are allowed. Junior Olympic/Coed/Men's Senior Play:
No metal spikes nor hard plastic or polyurethane
spikes similar to metal sole and heel plates are
allowed.

SECTION 7. ALL EQUIPMENT.

Notwithstanding the foregoing, the ASA reserves the
right to withhold or withdraw approval of any equipment which, in the ASA's sole determination, signifi-
cantly changes the character of the game, affects the
safety of participants or spectators, or renders a player's
performance more a product of the player's equipment
rather than the player's individual skill.

RULE 4 - PLAYERS AND SUBSTITUTES

SECTION 1. PLAYERS.

A. A team must have the required number of players present in the dugout or team area to start or continue a game. Players listed in the starting lineup and not available at game time may be substituted for and re-entered later.

   1. Official lineup sheets are to be completed and submitted to the official scorer or umpire at the start of each game. The lineup shall contain the first and last name, position and uniform number of each player.
NOTE: If a wrong number is on the lineup sheet, correct it and continue playing with no penalty. All available substitutes should be listed in the designated place by their last name, first name and uniform number.

   2. Eligible roster members may be added to the available substitute list at any time during the game.

B. Male rosters shall include only male players and female rosters shall include only female players.

C. A team shall consist of players in the following positions:

   1. Fast Pitch. Nine players: pitcher (F1), catcher (F2), first baseman (F3), second baseman (F4), third baseman (F5), shortstop (F6), left fielder (F7), center fielder (F8) and right fielder (F9).

   2. Fast Pitch with a Designated Player (DP). Ten players: same as fast pitch plus a DP.
NOTE: Refer to Section 3 DESIGNATED PLAYER for options resulting in nine players continuing the game.

3. Slow Pitch. Ten players: same as fast pitch plus an extra fielder (F10). **A game may begin with nine players, but when and if another player arrives, that player must be inserted into the lineup at the tenth batting position. Whenever a team is playing with only nine players, an out will be taken when the tenth position in the batting order appears. NOTE: Refer to Rule 4-1-D-2 Note for number of players to continue play under the shorthanded player rule. EXCEPTION: Coed Slow Pitch Play.**

4. Slow Pitch With An Extra Player (EP). Eleven players: same as slow pitch plus an EP who bats in the lineup. Seniors may have 11 or 12 players using one or two EPs.

5. Coed Slow Pitch. Ten players, (five male and five female) with the following positioning requirements: two males and two females in both the infield and the outfield, and one male and one female as pitcher and/or catcher. NOTE: If a team plays shorthanded with either three in the infield or outfield, at least one of the three must be a male and at least one of the three must be a female player.

6. Coed With Extra Players (EP). Twelve players, six male and six female—same as coed plus two EPs who bat in the lineup.

7. A physically challenged player can play offense or defense. (See Section 2)

D. **SHORT-HANDED RULE.**
   This rule may be used with the following requirements:
   1. If a team begins play with the required number of players as listed in C above, that team may continue a game with one less player than it

started with (slow pitch) or one less player than is currently in the lineup (fast pitch), whenever a player leaves the game for any reason other than ejection.

NOTE: Under no circumstances shall a team be permitted to bat less than nine (slow pitch) or eight (fast pitch).

2. If the player leaving the game is a runner (or batter), the runner or batter shall be declared out.

3. When the player who has left the game is scheduled to bat, an out shall be declared for each turn at bat.

NOTE: An inning or the game can end with an automatic out.

4. The player who has left the game cannot return to the lineup.

EXCEPTION: A player who has left the game under the blood rule (Rule 4, Section 8 B) may return even after missing a turn at bat.

EFFECT - Section 1 A-D: Failure to have the required number of eligible players to start or continue a game will result in a forfeiture.

SECTION 2. AMERICAN DISABILITY ACT RULE (Slow Pitch Only).

A. This rule may be used for a physically challenged person as determined by the American Disabilities Act passed on July 25, 1990. As a result of the player's disability, the player can play either offense or defense.

B. Teams using a physically challenged player on either offense or defense only must have 11 players. If the physically challenged player can play both, only 10 players are needed.

C. When a physically challenged person plays offense only, the team will follow the EP ruling as written.

There would be 11 hitters including the ADA player, and only 10 who play defense.

D. When a physically challenged player plays defense only, the player will be listed as the DEFO and placed last in the lineup. The team has the option to bat 10 or 11 players (if the EP is also used). When using a DEFO, it must be made known prior to the start of the game.

E. If a team starts the game with the DEFO option, the DEFO can never play offense. If this person for any reason cannot continue to play and the team has no other physically challenged player for a substitute, the EP can now play in his defensive position.

F. The DEFO position has the same re-entry status as any other starting position as long as the person substituted is also determined to be physically challenged under the ADA program. The original DEFO may re-enter only in the same spot on the lineup sheet.

G. If a DEFO or DEFOS, one male and/or one female, is used in the coed division, the name(s) must be inserted at the end of the lineup. The EP or two EPs can be listed anywhere in the first 10 positions. The batting order must still alternate as outlined in Rule 7, Section 2D and the defensive positioning remains as outlined in Rule 4, Section 1C.

NOTE: This special rule has been adopted to accommodate the athlete who is physically challenged. The intent is not to change the game and/or not to deprive any player from playing who would normally play, therefore, when using the EP, the normal EP rules will be followed including substitutions and re-entry. If the EP is used in addition to the DEFO, the DEFO must play defense and any of the other 11 players will be eligible to play defense. Only 11 are allowed to bat.

SECTION 3. DESIGNATED PLAYER (Fast Pitch Only).

    A. A designated player (DP) may be used for any player provided it is made known prior to the start of the game and the player's name is indicated on the lineup as one of the nine hitters in the batting order.

    B. The name of the player for whom the DP is batting (DEFO) will be placed in the 10th position in the lineup.

    C. The starting player listed as the DP must remain in the same position in the batting order for the entire game. The DP and the DP's substitute, or the substitute's replacement, may never play offense at the same time.

    D. The DP may be substituted for at any time, either by a pinch-hitter, pinch-runner or replaced by the defensive player for whom the DP is hitting (DEFO). If the starting DP is replaced on offense by the DEFO, the DP will leave the game. If replaced by a substitute, the DP position remains in the lineup. A starting DP may re-enter one time, as long as the DP returns to the original position in the batting order.

        1. If replaced by the person playing defense only (DEFO), this reduces the number of players from 10 to nine. If the DP does not re-enter, the game may legally end with nine players.

        2. If the DP re-enters and the DEFO was batting in the DP's spot, the DEFO can return to the number 10 position and play defense only or leave the game.

    E. The DP may play defense at any position. Should the DP play defense for a player other than the one for whom the DP is batting (DEFO), that player will continue to bat but not play defense, and is not considered to have left the game. The DP may play defense for the DEFO and the DEFO is considered to have left the game, reducing the number of players from 10 to nine.

F. The person being batted for (DEFO) may be substituted for at any time, either by a legal substitute or the DP for whom he is playing defense. The DEFO may re-enter the game one time, either in the number 10 position or in the DP's position in the batting order.

    1. If returning to the number 10 position, the DEFO will again play defense only but may play any defensive position.

    2. If the DEFO returns to the DP's position, the DEFO will play offense and defense; there will be only nine players in the batting order.

G. Placing the defensive player only (DEFO) into one of the first nine positions for someone other than the original DP is considered an **illegal batter**. The player is ejected.

NOTE: The DEFO replacing the DP is not a substitution, but the replacement should be reported to the umpire. There is no penalty for not reporting.

SECTION 4. EXTRA PLAYER (Slow Pitch Only).

A. An extra player (EP) is optional, but if one is used, it must be made known prior to the start of the game and be listed on the scoring sheet in the regular batting order. If the EP is used, the EP must be used the entire game. Failure to complete the game with 11 batters (12 in coed) as a result of an ejected player, results in a forfeiture of the game.

B. The EP must remain in the same position in the batting order for the entire game.

C. If an EP is used, all 11 on the starting lineup (12 in coed) must bat and any 10 of those 11 may play

defense. Defensive positions may be changed, but the
batting order must remain the same.

D. The EP may be substituted for at any time. The substitute must be a player who has not yet been in the
game. The starting EP may re-enter.

E. If the EP is used in coed, all 12 must bat and any 10,
(five male and five female), may play defense. Defensive positions may be changed as long as the coed
positioning is followed. The batting order must
remain the same throughout the game.

F. (Men's Senior Only). One or two extra players may
be designated at any place in the batting order. The
EP(s) may enter a game on defense at any time, but
the batting order must remain the same throughout
the game.

SECTION 5. RE-ENTRY.

A. Any of the starting players, including a DP and DEFO
(Fast Pitch Only) or an EP (Slow Pitch Only), may be
substituted or replaced and re-entered once, provided
players occupy the original positions whenever in the
lineup.

B. **Non starting players may not re-enter. Starting players may not re-enter a second time. The starting
player and his substitute may not be in the lineup at
the same time.**

C. **If a non starting player re-enters the game, a starting
player re-enters the game a second time or a starting
player re-enters the game in a position in the lineup
other than their original starting position, this is considered an illegal re-entry.**

D. Violation of re-entry rule is handled as a protest when
brought to the attention of the umpire by the offended
team and may be made anytime while the player is in
the game.

EFFECT - Section 5 A-C: The illegal player shall be ejected. **The position in the lineup where the player entered illegally shall be filled by a substitute. For determining when a batter is called out, when runners return and when managers are given an option, the penalties for unreported or illegal substitution are in effect.**

SECTION 6. SUBSTITUTES.

A substitute may take the place of a player whose name is in his team's batting order. The following regulations govern player substitutions:

A. The manager or team representative of the team making the substitution shall immediately notify the plate umpire at the time a substitute enters. The plate umpire shall then report the change to the scorer prior to the next pitch. If the violation is discovered prior to a pitch being made (legal or illegal), there is no penalty and the illegal substitute shall be declared legal.

B. Substitute players will be considered in the game when reported to the plate umpire. A player will not violate the substitution rule until one legal or illegal pitch has been thrown. The use of an illegal substitute is handled as a protest by the offended team while the player is in the game. If the team manager or player in violation informs the umpire prior to the offended team's protest, there is no violation regardless of how long the player or players were illegally in the game.

    1. **OFFENSE.** If the illegal player is discovered by the defense before the offensive manager, coach or player in violation informs the umpire and:

        (a) after one legal or illegal pitch has been thrown while the illegal player is at bat, the illegal player is ejected and a legal substitute assumes the ball and strike

count. Any advance of runners while the
illegal batter is at bat is legal.

(b) the illegal player has completed a turn at
bat and prior to the next legal or illegal
pitch, or before the defensive team has
left the field, the illegal player is called
out, ejected and any advance of runners
as a result of the illegal batter becoming a
batter-runner is nullified.

(c) he has completed his turn at bat and after
the next legal or illegal pitch, or after the
defensive team has left the field, the illegal player is ejected and if on base
replaced by a legal substitute and any
advance by runners while the illegal batter was at bat as a result of his becoming a
batter-runner is legal.

(d) if the player is in the game illegally as a runner, the player is ejected and replaced on
base by a legal substitute or the starting
player re-enters.

(e) **placing an offensive player in the lineup as
a runner for another offensive player, or
placing the DEFO in the lineup as a runner for another offensive player is considered an illegal runner. The player is
ejected.**

EXCEPTION: Men's Senior Slow Pitch.

2. **DEFENSE.** If the illegal player is discovered by
the offense before the defensive manager, coach
or player in violation informs the umpire and:

(a) after the illegal palyer makes a play and
prior to the next legal or illegal pitch,
before the defensive team has left the

field, or on the last play of the game before the umpires have left the field, the offensive team has the option of taking the result of the play or having the last batter return and assume the ball and strike count the batter had prior to the discovery of the illegal player with each runner returning to the base which was occupied prior to the play. The illegal player is ejected.

(b) after a legal or illegal pitch to the next batter, all play stands but the illegal player is ejected.

3. **ILLEGAL PITCHER. A player removed from the pitching position by the umpire cannot return to pitch. Placing a removed pitcher back into the pitching position is considered an illegal pitcher. The player is ejected and all play stands.**

C. Any player, including the pitcher, may be removed from the game during any dead ball.

NOTE: The pitcher is not required to pitch until the first batter facing him has completed his turn at bat or the other side has been retired.

D. If an accident to a batter-runner prevents him from proceeding to an awarded base, and the ball is dead, the batter-runner or runner may be replaced with a legal substitute. This player will be allowed to proceed to any awarded base(s). This player must legally touch any awarded or missed bases not previously touched, or any base left before a fly ball was first contacted.

NOTE: This is not a courtesy runner, but a legal sub-stitute.

SECTION 7. EJECTED PLAYER.

A player or coach who has been ejected from the game is restricted to the bench unless the act is determined to be flagrant, when the player or coach must leave the grounds. Any ejected player discovered participating will constitute a forfeit.

SECTION 8. BLOOD RULE.

A player, coach or umpire who is bleeding or who has blood on his uniform shall be prohibited from participating further in the game until appropriate treatment can be administered. If medical care or treatment is administered in a reasonable length of time, the individual will not have to leave the game. The length of time that is considered reasonable is left to the umpire's judgment. Uniform rule violations will not be enforced if a uniform change is required. The umpire shall:

A. Stop the game and immediately call a coach, trainer, or other authorized person to the injured player and allow treatment.

B. Apply the rules of the game regarding substitution, short-handed player and re-entry if necessary.

RULE 5 - THE GAME

SECTION 1. HOME TEAM.

The team designated as home team shall bat last in the inning.

SECTION 2. FITNESS OF THE GROUND.

The fitness of the ground for a game shall be decided solely by the plate umpire.

SECTION 3. REGULATION GAME.

A. A regulation game shall consist of seven innings. A full seven innings need not be played if the team second at bat scores more runs in six and one-half innings and/or before the third out in the last of the seventh inning, or the run ahead rule is applied.

B. A game that is tied at the end of seven innings shall be continued by playing additional innings until one side has scored more runs than the other at the end of a complete inning, or until the team second at bat has scored more runs in their half of the inning before the third out is made.

C. A game called by the umpire shall be regulation if five or more complete innings have been played, or if the team second at bat has scored more runs in four or more innings than the other team has scored in five or more innings. The umpire is empowered to call a game at any time because of darkness, rain, fire, panic or other causes which place the patrons or players in peril. (For ASA national tournament play, see ASA Code 209 B)

D. Games that are not considered regulation shall be resumed at the exact point where they were stopped.

E. A regulation tie game shall be declared if the score is equal when the game is called at the end of five or

more complete innings, or if the team second at bat
has equaled the score of the first team at bat in the
incomplete inning.

F. Games that are regulation tie games shall be resumed
at the exact point where they were stopped.

SECTION 4. FORFEITED GAMES.

A forfeited game shall be declared by the umpire in favor
of the team not at fault in the following cases:

A. If an umpire is physically attacked by any team member and/or spectator.

B. If a team fails to appear on the field, or, being on the
field, refuses to begin a game for which it is scheduled
or assigned within a time set for forfeitures by the
organization which the team represents.

C. If one side refuses to continue to play after the game
has begun, unless the game has been suspended or terminated by the umpire.

D. If, after play has been suspended by the umpire, one
side fails to resume playing within two minutes after
"play ball" has been declared by the umpire.

E. If a team employs tactics noticeably designed to delay
or to hasten the game.

F. If, after warning by the umpire, any one of the rules
of the game is willfully violated.

G. If the order for the ejection of a player is not obeyed
within one minute.

H. If the ejection of a player or players from the game
results in fewer than the required number of players
to continue the game.

I.   If an ejected player is discovered participating again.

J.   If a team is playing one player short and another
player becomes injured or ill, leaving the team with
two less players than the required number.

SECTION 5. SCORING OF RUNS.

A. One run shall be scored each time a runner touches first, second or third bases and home plate.

B. No run shall be scored if the third out of the inning is the result of:

1. A batter-runner being called out prior to reaching first base or any other runner forced out due to the batter becoming a batter-runner.

2. A runner being put out by a tag or live ball appeal play prior to the lead runner touching home plate.

3. A preceding runner is declared out on an appeal play.

   NOTE: An appeal can be made after the third out in order to nullify a run.

SECTION 6. GAME WINNER.

The winner of the game shall be the team that scores more runs in a regulation game.

A. The score of a called regulation game shall be the score at the end of the last complete inning, unless the team second at bat has scored an equal number or more runs than the first team at bat in the incomplete inning. In this case, the score shall be that of the incomplete inning.

B. The score of a regulation tie game shall be the tie score when the game was terminated.

   (NOTE: See Rule 5, Section 3F regarding resumption of play.)

C. The score of a forfeited game shall be seven to zero in favor of the team not at fault.

SECTION 7. CONFERENCES.

A. **Offensive Conference.** There shall be only one charged conference between the manager and/or other team representative(s) and the batter and/or runner(s) in an inning. The umpire shall not permit any such conferences in excess of one in an inning.

EFFECT: Ejection of the manager or coach who insists on another charged conference.

B. **Defensive Conference.** There shall be only one charged conference between the manager or other team representative from the dugout with each pitcher in an inning.

EFFECT: The second charged conference shall result in the removal of the pitcher from the pitching position for the remainder of the game.

PENALTY: If the pitcher returns to the pitcher's position at any time during the game after two defensive conferences in the same inning, the pitcher is ejected from the game. The removed pitcher can play another position on defense but cannot pitch again.

NOTE: If a pitcher is removed from the pitching position after one conference, and returns to pitch in the same inning, conferences do not start over. The pitcher would still be removed if a second conference is requested in the same inning.

C. **(Super Slow Pitch Only) There shall be only three (3) charged conferences between the manager or other team representative from the dugout with ANY defensive player(s) during the game.**

EFFECT: Each conference after the third shall result in the pitcher being removed from the pitching position for the remainder of the game.

SECTION 8. HOME RUN RULE (Slow Pitch Only) (Code Article 209 I).

A limit of over-the-fence home runs will be used in all men's and coed slow pitch divisions. All balls hit over the fence by a team in excess of the following limitations per game will be ruled on as shown:

A. **Super Classification.** Unlimited.

B. **Major, Major Industrial, and Major Church Classifications.** Twelve. The batter is ruled out for any in excess.

C. **Major Masters Classification. Nine. The batter is ruled out for any in excess. (Beginning 1999)**

D. **Class A Classification.** Six. The batter is ruled out for any in excess.

E. **Major Coed Classification.** Five. The batter is ruled out for any in excess.
   NOTE: Both male and female home runs count toward the limit.

F. **Class B, Class A Industrial, Class A Church, and all Masters and Seniors Classifications.** Three. The batter is ruled out for any in excess.
   (NOTE: Class A Masters beginning in 1999).

G. **Class A Coed Classification.** Two. The first batter hitting a home run in excess of two is ruled out and all other players hitting a home run are ruled out and disqualified from the game.
   NOTE: Both male and female home runs count toward the limit.

H. **Class C Classification.** One. The first batter hitting a home run in excess of one is ruled out and all other players hitting a home run are ruled out and disqualified from the game.

I. **Class D Classification.** None. The batter is ruled out for the first in excess and all other players hitting a home run are ruled out and disqualified from the game.
   NOTE (A-H):
   1. Any fair fly ball touched by a defensive player which then goes over the fence in fair territory, should be declared a four-base award and shall not be included in the total of over-the-fence home runs.

2. Any time the batter is ruled out because of the excessive home run rule, the ball is dead and no runners can advance.

3. A home run will be charged for any ball hit over the fence whether runs score or not.

4. A substitute can be entered for a disqualified player. If no substitutes are available, a team can play one player short. (See Rule 4, Section 1D) NOTE: A team cannot play two players short. A forfeit would be ruled if two players short.

SECTION 9. RUN AHEAD RULE (Code Article 209 F).

A. A run ahead rule must be used after five innings at all National Tournaments.

EXCEPTION: Men's Super Slow Pitch

1. Fast Pitch - 8.
2. Modified Pitch - 10.
3. Slow Pitch - **20 after four innings** or 12 after five innings.
4. Super Slow Pitch - 20 after four innings or 15 after five innings.

B. Complete innings must be played unless the home team scores the run ahead limit while at bat. Whenever a run ahead limit is used and the visiting team reaches the limit in the fifth or sixth inning, the home team must have their opportunity to bat in the bottom half of the inning.

SECTION 10. TIME LIMIT RULE
(Code Article 209 G).
In all Junior Olympic Class A and Gold Pool play, no inning shall start after 1 hour and 40 minutes. If the game is still tied after the time limit has expired, the tie breaker shall be in effect at the start of the next inning.

SECTION 11. TIE-BREAKER (Code Article 209 H).
(Women and Junior Olympic Girls Fast Pitch Only)

If, after the completion of nine innings of play, the score is tied, the following tie-breaker will be played to determine a winning team.

A. Starting with the top of the tenth inning, and each half inning thereafter, the offensive team shall begin its turn at bat with the player who is scheduled to bat last in that respective half inning being placed on second base (e.g., if the number five batter is the lead off batter, the number four batter in the batting order will be placed on second base. A substitute may be inserted for the runner.) For scoring, see Rule 11, Section 10.

NOTE: If a team is in the tiebreaker and the absent player is the one who should begin the half inning at second base, do not declare an out. Instead, place on second base the player whose name precedes the absent player's name in the lineup.

SECTION 12. DUGOUT CONDUCT.

Coaches, players, substitutes, or other bench personnel shall not be outside the designated bench dugout area except when the rule allows or justified by the umpire.

EFFECT: The first offense is a team warning. Any repeat offense shall result in the ejection of that team member.

RULE 6 - PITCHING REGULATIONS (Fast Pitch)

SECTION 1. PRELIMINARIES.

Before starting the delivery (pitch), the pitcher shall comply with the following:

A. Both feet must be on the ground within the 24-inch length of the pitcher's plate. The shoulders shall be in line with first and third bases.

   1. (Male Only) He shall take a position with his pivot foot in contact with the pitcher's plate and his non-pivot foot on or behind the pitcher's plate.

   2. (Female Only) She shall take a position with both feet in contact with the pitcher's plate.

B. **While on the pitching plate,** the pitcher shall take the signal **or appear to be taking a signal** with the hands separated. The ball must remain in either the glove or pitching hand.

C. The pitcher shall hold the ball in both hands for not less than one second and not more than 10 seconds before releasing it.

   1. (Male Only) If the pitcher decides to pitch with the non-pivot foot to the rear and off the pitching plate, the backward step may be taken before, simultaneous with or after the hands are brought together. The pivot foot must remain in contact with the pitching plate at all times prior to the forward step.

   2. (Female Only) Both feet must remain in contact with the pitching plate at all times prior to the forward step.

D. The pitcher shall not be considered in the pitching position unless the catcher is in position to receive the pitch.

E. The pitcher may not take the pitching position on or near the pitcher's plate without having the ball in his possession.

SECTION 2. STARTING THE PITCH.

The pitch starts when one hand is taken off the ball after the hands have been placed together.

SECTION 3. LEGAL DELIVERY.

A. The pitcher must not make any motion to pitch without immediately delivering the ball to the batter.

B. The pitcher must not use a pitching motion in which, after having the ball in both hands in the pitching position, the pitcher removes one hand from the ball, and returns the ball to both hands in front of the body.

C. The pitcher must not make a stop or reversal of the forward motion after separating the hands.

D. The pitcher must not make two revolutions of the arm on the windmill pitch. A pitcher may drop the arm to the side and to the rear before starting the windmill motion.

E. The delivery must be an underhanded motion with the hand below the hip and the wrist not farther from the body than the elbow.

F. The release of the ball and follow through of the hand and wrist must be forward and past the straight line of the body.

G. In the act of delivering the ball, the pitcher must take one step with the non-pivot foot simultaneous with the release of the ball. The step must be forward and toward the batter within the 24-inch length of the pitcher's plate.

NOTE: It is not a step if the pitcher slides the pivot foot across the pitcher's plate, provided contact is maintained with the plate. Raising the foot off the

pitching plate and returning it to the plate creates a rocking motion and is an illegal act.

H. Pushing off with the pivot foot from a place other than the pitcher's plate is illegal. This includes a "crow hop" as defined under Rule 1.

I. **(All Female and Junior Olympic Boys Only)** The pivot foot must remain in contact with or push off and drag away from the pitching plate prior to the front foot touching the ground, as long as the pivot foot remains in contact with the ground.

J. **(Adult Male Only)** Both feet can be in the air at the same time. The leap is legal as long as the pivot foot does not replant and push off from a spot other than the pitching plate.

K. The pitcher must not make another revolution after releasing the ball.

L. The pitcher shall not deliberately drop, roll or bounce the ball in order to prevent the batter from hitting it.

M. The pitcher has 20 seconds to release the next pitch after receiving the ball or after the umpire indicates "play ball."

SECTION 4. INTENTIONAL WALK.

If the pitcher desires to walk a batter intentionally all pitches must be legally delivered to the batter. A pitchout for the purpose of intentionally walking a batter is not considered an illegal pitch.

SECTION 5. DEFENSIVE POSITIONING.

A. The pitcher shall not deliver a pitch unless all defensive players are positioned in fair territory, except the catcher who must be in the catcher's box.

B. A fielder shall not take a position in the batter's line of vision or, with deliberate unsportsmanlike intent, act in a manner to distract the batter. A pitch does not have to be released.

NOTE: The offending player shall also be ejected from the game.

C. The catcher or any other fielder shall not step on or in front of home plate without the ball, or on a swing or attempted bunt, touch the batter or his bat with a runner on third base trying to score by means of a squeeze play or a steal.

NOTE: The batter shall also be awarded first base on the obstruction and the ball is dead. For batter interferences see Rule 7-6N.

SECTION 6. FOREIGN SUBSTANCE.

Any defensive player shall not at any time during the game be allowed to use any foreign substance upon the ball. Under the supervision and control of the umpire, powdered resin may be used to dry the hands. The pitcher shall not wear tape on his fingers, a sweatband, bracelet, or similar type item on the wrist or forearm of the pitching arm.

NOTE: Batting gloves may not be worn on the pitching hand.

EFFECT: An illegal pitch shall be called on the first offense. If any defensive player continues to place a foreign substance on the ball, the player should be ejected from the ball game.

SECTION 7. CATCHER.

A. The catcher must remain within the lines of the catcher's box until the pitch is released.

B. The catcher shall return the ball directly to the pitcher after each pitch, except after a strikeout, a putout or an attempted putout made by the catcher.

EXCEPTION: Does not apply with a runner(s) on base or the batter becoming a batter-runner.

SECTION 8. THROWING TO A BASE.

The pitcher shall not throw to a base during a live ball while either foot is in contact with the pitcher's plate after the pitcher has taken the pitching position. If the throw from the pitcher's plate occurs during a live ball appeal play, the appeal is canceled.

NOTE: The pitcher may move back from the pitching position by stepping backwards off the pitcher's plate prior to separating his hands. Stepping forward or sideways at any time constitutes an illegal pitch.

EFFECT - Sections 1-8:

Any infraction of Sections 1-8 is an illegal pitch.
EFFECT:

A. The umpire shall give a delayed dead ball signal.
B. If the batter hits the ball and reaches first base safely, and if all other runners have advanced at least one base on the batted ball, the illegal pitch is cancelled. All action as a result of the batted ball stands. No option is given.
C. Otherwise the manager has the option to take the result of the play, or the illegal pitch is enforced by awarding a ball to the batter (if ball four award first base) and advancing all runners one base.
NOTE: If an illegal pitch hits the batter, the batter is awarded first base and all runners are awarded one base.

SECTION 9. WARM-UP PITCHES.

At the beginning of each half inning, or when a pitcher relieves another, not more than one minute may be used to deliver not more than five pitches. Play shall be suspended during this time. For excessive warm-up pitches, a pitcher shall be penalized by awarding a ball to the batter for each pitch in excess of five. This does not apply if the umpire delays the start of play due to substitution, conference, injuries, etc.

NOTE: A pitcher returning to pitch in the same half inning will not receive warm-up pitches.

NOTE: There is no limitation as to the number of times a player can return to the pitching position if the player has not left the batting order or has not been removed from the pitcher's position by the umpire.

SECTION 10. NO PITCH.

No pitch shall be declared when:

A. The pitcher pitches during the suspension of play.

B. The pitcher attempts a quick return of the ball before the batter has taken a position in the batter's box or when the batter is off balance as a result of a previous pitch.

C. A runner is called out for leaving a base prior to the pitcher releasing the ball.

D. The pitcher pitches before a runner has retouched his base after being legitimately off that base.

E. No player, manager or coach shall call time, employ any other word or phrase, or commit any act while the ball is alive and in play for the obvious purpose of trying to make the pitcher commit an illegal pitch.
   NOTE: A warning shall be issued to the offending team, and a repeat of this type act by any member of the team warned shall result in the offender being ejected from the game.

EFFECT - Section 10 A-E:

The ball is dead, and all subsequent action on that pitch is canceled.

SECTION 11. DROPPED BALL.

If the ball slips from the pitcher's hand during the delivery, a ball is declared on the batter, the ball will remain in play and the runners may advance at their own risk.

RULE 6 -
PITCHING REGULATIONS (Modified Pitch)

SECTION 1. PRELIMINARIES.

Before starting the delivery (pitch), the pitcher shall comply with the following:

A. The pitcher shall take a position with both feet in contact with the pitcher's plate. Both feet must be on the ground within the 24-inch length of the pitcher's plate. The shoulders shall be in line with first and third bases.

B. **While on the pitcher's plate,** the pitcher shall take a signal, **or appear to be taking a signal,** with the hands separated. The ball must remain in the glove or pitching hand.

C. The pitcher shall hold the ball in both hands for not less than one second and not more than 10 seconds before releasing it.

D. The pitcher shall not be considered in pitching position unless the catcher is in position to receive the pitch.

E. The pitcher may not take the pitching position on or near the pitcher's plate without having the ball in possession.

SECTION 2. STARTING THE PITCH.

The pitch starts when one hand is taken off the ball after the hands have been placed together.

SECTION 3. LEGAL DELIVERY.

A. The pitcher must not make any motion to pitch without immediately delivering the ball to the batter.

B. The pitcher must not use a pitching motion in which, after having the ball in both hands in the pitching position, the pitcher removes one hand from the ball and returns the ball to both hands.

C. The pitcher shall not make a stop or reversal of the forward motion after separating the hands.

D. The pitcher may take the ball behind the back on the back swing.

E. The pitcher must not use a windmill or slingshot-type pitch or make a complete revolution in the delivery.

F. Position of the ball:

   1. (Major) No restriction on the backward swing or on the downward motion and during the complete delivery.

   2. ("A") No restriction on the backward swing or at the top of the backswing. The ball must not be outside the pitcher's wrist on the downward motion and during the complete delivery.

   3. (10-Man) The ball must not be outside the pitcher's wrist on the backswing, at the top of the backswing, on the downward motion, or during the complete delivery.

G. The delivery must be underhanded motion with the hand below the hip and the pitcher's palm may be pointing downward.

H. Arm, shoulder, hip:

   1. (Major) No restrictions on the arm. The shoulders and driving hip must be squared to home plate when the ball is released.

   2. ("A" and 10-Man) On the forward swing of the pitching arm, the elbow must be locked at the point of release and the shoulders and driving hip must be squared to home plate when the ball is released.

I. The release of the ball must be on the first forward swing of the pitching arm past the hip. The release must have a complete, smooth follow-through with no abrupt stop of the arm near the hip.

J. In the act of delivering the ball, the pitcher must take
one step simultaneous with the release of the ball. The
step must be forward and toward the batter within the
24-inch length of the pitcher's plate.
NOTE: It is not a step if the pitcher slides the pivot
foot across the pitcher's plate, provided contact is
maintained with the plate. Raising the foot off the
pitching plate and returning it to the plate creates a
rocking motion and is an illegal act.

K. Pushing off with the pivot foot from a place other
than the pitcher's plate is illegal.

L. The pitcher shall not deliberately drop, roll or bounce
the ball in order to prevent the batter from hitting it.

M. The pitcher has 20 seconds to release the next pitch
after receiving the ball or after the umpire indicates
"play ball".

SECTION 4. INTENTIONAL WALK.

If the pitcher desires to walk a batter intentionally all
pitches must be legally delivered to the batter. A pitchout
for the purpose of intentionally walking a batter is not
considered an illegal pitch.

SECTION 5. DEFENSIVE POSITIONING.

A. The pitcher shall not deliver a pitch unless all defensive players are positioned in fair territory, except the
catcher who must be in the catcher's box.

B. A fielder shall not take a position in the batter's line of
vision or, with deliberate unsportsmanlike intent, act
in a manner to distract the batter. A pitch does not
have to be released.
NOTE: The offending player shall also be ejected from
the game.

C. The catcher or any other fielder shall not step on or in
front of home plate without the ball, or touch the bat-

ter or the bat with a runner on third base trying to
score by means of a squeeze play or a steal.

NOTE: The batter shall also be awarded first base on
the obstruction and the ball is dead.

SECTION 6. FOREIGN SUBSTANCE.

Any defensive player shall not, at any time during the
game, be allowed to use any foreign substance upon the
ball. Under the supervision and control of the umpire,
powdered resin may be used to dry the hands. The
pitcher shall not wear tape on the fingers, a sweatband,
bracelet, or similar type item on the wrist or forearm of
the pitching arm.

NOTE: Batting gloves may not be worn on the pitching
hand.

EFFECT: An illegal pitch shall be called on the first
offense. If any defensive player continues to place a foreign substance on the ball, the player should be ejected
from the ball game.

SECTION 7. CATCHER.

A. The catcher must remain within the lines of the
catcher's box until the pitch is released.

B. The catcher shall return the ball directly to the pitcher
after each pitch, except after a strikeout, put out or an
attempted put out made by the catcher.

EXCEPTION: Does not apply with a runner(s) on
base or the batter becoming a batter-runner.

SECTION 8. THROWING TO A BASE.

The pitcher shall not throw to a base during a live ball
while either foot is in contact with the pitcher's plate after
the pitcher has taken the pitching position. If the throw
from the pitcher's plate occurs during a live ball appeal
play, the appeal is canceled.

NOTE: The pitcher may move back from the pitching

position by stepping backwards off the pitcher's plate prior to separating his hands. Stepping forward or sideways at any time constitutes an illegal pitch.

EFFECT - Sections 1-8:

Any infraction of Sections 1-8 is an illegal pitch.
EFFECT:

A. The umpire shall give a delayed dead ball signal.
B. If the batter hits the ball and reaches first base safely, and if all other runners have advanced at least one base on the batted ball, the illegal pitch is cancelled. All action as a result of the batted ball stands. No option is given.
C. Otherwise the manager has the option to take the result of the play, or the illegal pitch is enforced by awarding a ball to the batter (if ball four award first base) and advancing all runners one base.
NOTE: If an illegal pitch hits the batter, the batter is awarded first base and all runners are awarded one base.

SECTION 9. WARM-UP PITCHES.

At the beginning of each half inning, or when a pitcher relieves another, not more than one minute may be used to deliver not more than three pitches. Play shall be suspended during this time. For excessive warm-up pitches, a pitcher shall be penalized by awarding a ball to the batter for each pitch in excess of three. This does not apply if the umpire delays the start of play due to substitution, conference, injuries, etc. NOTE: A pitcher returning to pitch in the same half inning will not receive warm-up pitches. There is no limitation as to the number of times a player can return to the pitching position if the player has not left the batting order or has not been removed from the pitcher's position by the umpire.

SECTION 10. NO PITCH.

No pitch shall be declared when:

A. The pitcher pitches during the suspension of play.

B. The pitcher attempts a quick return of the ball before the batter has taken a position in the batter's box or when the batter is off balance as a result of a previous pitch.

C. A runner is called out for leaving a base prior to the pitcher releasing the pitch.

D. The pitcher pitches before a runner has returned to the base after being legitimately off that base.

E. No player, manager or coach shall call time, employ any other word or phrase, or commit any act while the ball is alive and in play for the obvious purpose of trying to make the pitcher commit an illegal pitch.
NOTE: A warning shall be issued to the offending team, and a repeat of this type act by any member of the team warned shall result in the offender being ejected from the game.

EFFECT - Section 10 A-E:
The ball is dead, and all subsequent action on that pitch is canceled.

SECTION 11. DROPPED BALL.

If the ball slips from the pitcher's hand during the delivery, a ball is declared on the batter, the ball will remain in play and the runners may advance at their own risk.

RULE 6 - PITCHING REGULATIONS (Slow Pitch)

SECTION 1. PRELIMINARIES.

A. The pitcher must take a position with both feet firmly on the ground and with one or both feet in contact with the pitcher's plate. The pitcher's pivot foot must be in contact with the pitcher's plate throughout the delivery.

B. The pitcher must come to a full and complete stop with the ball in front of the body. The front of the body must face the batter. This position must be maintained at least one second before starting the delivery.

C. The pitcher shall not be considered in the pitching position unless the catcher is in position to receive the pitch.

D. The pitcher must not make any motion to pitch while in contact with the pitcher's plate.
   NOTE: A dead ball should be called, an illegal pitch ruled, a warning is issued, and repeated action would result in the pitcher ruled illegal, and removed from the pitching position.

SECTION 2. STARTING THE PITCH.

The pitch starts when the pitcher makes any motion **with the ball** that is part of the delivery after the required stop. **While on the pitching plate** prior to the required stop, any motion may be used.

SECTION 3. LEGAL DELIVERY.

A. The pitcher must not make any motion to pitch without immediately delivering the ball to the batter.

B. The delivery is a continuous motion.

C. The pitcher must not use a delivery in which there is a stop or reversal of the pitching motion.

D. The pitcher must deliver the ball toward home plate on the first forward swing of the pitching arm past the hip with an underhanded motion.

E. The pivot foot must remain in contact with the pitcher's plate until the pitched ball leaves the hand. If a step is taken, it can be forward, backward, or to the side, provided the pivot foot is in contact with the pitcher's plate and the step is simultaneous with the release of the ball.

F. The pitcher must not pitch the ball behind the back or through the legs.

G. The pitch shall be released at a moderate speed. The speed is left entirely up to the judgment of the umpire. The umpire shall warn the pitcher who delivers a pitch with excessive speed. If the pitcher repeats such an act after being warned, the pitcher shall be removed from the pitcher's position for the remainder of the game.

H. The ball must be delivered with perceptible arc and reach a height of at least six feet (1.83m) from the ground, while not exceeding a maximum height of 12 feet (3.66m) from the ground.

I. The pitcher must not continue the pitching motion after he releases the ball.

J. The pitcher has 10 seconds to release the next pitch after receiving the ball, or after the umpire indicates "play ball".

K. The pitcher shall not deliver a pitch from the glove.

SECTION 4. DEFENSIVE POSITIONING.

A. The pitcher shall not deliver a pitch unless all defensive players are positioned in fair territory, except the catcher who must be in the catcher's box.

B. A fielder shall not take a position in the batter's line of vision or, with deliberate unsportsmanlike intent, act in a manner to distract the batter. A pitch does not have to be released.

NOTE: The offending player shall also be ejected from the game.

SECTION 5. FOREIGN SUBSTANCE.

Any defensive player shall not, at any time during the game, be allowed to use any foreign substance upon the ball, the pitching hand or the fingers. Under the supervision and control of the umpire, powdered resin may be used to dry the hands. The pitcher may wear tape on the fingers or a sweatband on the wrist or forearm of the pitching arm.

NOTE: Batting gloves may not be worn on the pitching hand.

EFFECT: An illegal pitch shall be called on the first offense. If any defensive player continues to place a foreign substance on the ball, the player should be ejected from the ball game.

SECTION 6. CATCHER.

A. The catcher must remain within the lines of the catcher's box until the pitched ball is batted, touches the ground or plate, or reaches the catcher's box.

B. The catcher shall return the ball directly to the pitcher after each pitch, except after a strikeout.

EXCEPTION: (Super Slow Pitch)

EFFECT: An additional ball is awarded to the batter.

SECTION 7. QUICK PITCH.

The pitcher shall not attempt a quick return of the ball before the batter has taken a position in the batter's box or when the batter is off balance as a result of a pitch.

EFFECT —Sections 1-7:

Any infraction of Sections 1-7 is an illegal pitch. A ball shall be called on the batter. Runners are not advanced.

EXCEPTION: If a batter swings at or contacts any illegal pitch, it is nullified and all play stands.

SECTION 8. WARM-UP PITCHES.

At the beginning of each half inning, or when a pitcher relieves another, not more than one minute may be used to deliver not more than three warm-up pitches. Play shall be suspended during this time. For excessive warm-up pitches, a pitcher shall be penalized by awarding a ball to the batter for each pitch. This does not apply if umpire delays the start of play due to substitution, conference, injuries, etc.

NOTE: A pitcher returning to pitch in the same half inning will not receive warm-up pitches.

SECTION 9. NO PITCH.

No pitch shall be declared when:

A. The pitcher pitches during the suspension of play.

B. A runner is called out for leaving a base before the pitched ball reaches home plate, is batted, or touches the ground before reaching home plate.

C. The pitcher pitches before a runner has returned to base after a foul ball has been declared and the ball is dead.

D. **The pitcher pitches before a runner has retouched his base after being legitimately off that base.**

E. The ball slips from the pitcher's hand during the windup or during the back swing.

F. No player, manager or coach shall call time, employ any other word or phrase, or commit any act while the ball is alive and in play for the obvious purpose of trying to make the pitcher commit an illegal pitch.

NOTE: A warning shall be issued to the offending team, and a repeat of this type act by any member of the team warned shall result in the offender being removed from the game.

EFFECT: Section 9 A-F:

The ball is dead, and all subsequent action on that pitch is canceled.

RULE 6 -
PITCHING REGULATIONS (16-Inch Slow Pitch)

SECTION 1. PRELIMINARIES.

A. The pitcher must take a position with both feet firmly on the ground and with one or both feet in contact with the pitcher's plate. The pitcher's pivot foot must be in contact with the pitcher's plate throughout the delivery.

B. The pitcher must come to a complete stop with the ball in front of the body. The front of the body must face the batter. This position must be maintained at least one second before starting the delivery.

C. The pitcher shall not be considered in pitching position unless the catcher is in position to receive the pitch.

D. While the pitcher is in the pitching position, in the motion for the delivery, or in the act of faking a delivery prior to a hesitation, the pivot foot must be in contact with the pitcher's plate. After a hesitation, the foot may leave the pitcher's plate during an attempted pickoff or a fake throw. When the pitching motion is restarted, the restriction takes effect again.

E. The pitcher may not take the pitching position on or near the pitcher's plate without having the ball in his possession.

SECTION 2. STARTING THE PITCH.

The pitch starts when the pitcher makes any motion with the ball that is part of the delivery after the required stop. While on the pitching plate, prior to the required stop, any motion may be used.

SECTION 3. LEGAL DELIVERY.

A. The pivot foot must remain in contact with the pitcher's plate until the pitched ball leaves the hand. If a step is taken, it can be forward, backward, or to the side, provided the pivot foot is in contact with the pitcher's plate and the step is simultaneous with the release of the ball.

B. The pitcher must not pitch the ball behind the back or through the legs.

C. The pitch shall be released at a moderate speed. The speed is left entirely up to the judgment of the umpire. The umpire shall warn the pitcher who delivers a pitch with excessive speed. If the pitcher repeats such an act after being warned, the pitcher shall be removed from the pitcher's position for the remainder of the game.

D. The ball must be delivered with a perceptible arc and reach a height of at least six feet (1.83m) from the ground, while not exceeding a maximum height of 12 feet (3.66m) from the ground.

E. The pitcher must not continue his motion after releasing the ball.

F. The pitcher must not commit a third hesitation before the mandatory delivery of a pitch, legal or illegal. Hesitations are defined as:

1. Making any motion to pitch without immediately delivering the ball to the batter.

2. Using a delivery which is not a continuous motion.

3. Using a delivery in which there is a stop or reversal of the pitching motion.

4. Not delivering the ball toward home plate on the first forward swing of the pitching arm past the hip.

NOTE:

(a) After a hesitation of the pitching motion, and before a restart of the motion, the pitcher may attempt or fake a throw for a pickoff with the pivot foot in contact with the pitcher's plate.

(b) Runners may be off the bases without penalty during the delivery or fake delivery.

(c) During the pickoff attempt of the pitcher, or the catcher following a pitch, each runner must return to the base occupied at the start of the pitch, and before the runner is touched with the ball.

(d) If the ball is overthrown, no runners may advance.

(e) If the thrown ball remains in playable territory, the runners are in jeopardy until they return to their original bases.

G. The pitcher has 10 seconds to release the next pitch after receiving the ball, or after the umpire indicates "play ball."

H. The pitcher shall not deliver a pitch from the glove.

SECTION 4. DEFENSIVE POSITIONING.

A. The pitcher shall not deliver a pitch unless all defensive players are positioned in fair territory, except the catcher who must be in the catcher's box.

B. A fielder shall not take a position in the batter's line of vision or, with deliberate unsportsmanlike intent, act in a manner to distract the batter. A pitch does not have to be released.

NOTE: The offending player shall also be ejected from the game.

SECTION 5. FOREIGN SUBSTANCE.

Any defensive player shall not, at any time during the game, be allowed to use any foreign substance upon the ball. Under the supervision and control of the umpire, powdered resin may be used to dry the hands. The pitcher may wear tape on the fingers or a sweatband on the wrist or forearm of the pitching arm. Batting gloves may not be worn on the pitching hand.

EFFECT: An illegal pitch shall be called on the first offense. If any defensive player continues to place a foreign substance on the ball, the player should be ejected from the ball game.

SECTION 6. CATCHER.

A. The catcher must remain within the lines of the catcher's box until the pitched ball is batted, touches the ground or plate, or reaches the catcher's box.

B. The catcher shall return the ball directly to the pitcher after each pitch, except after a strikeout.

EFFECT: An additional ball is awarded to the batter.

EXCEPTION: Does not apply when the batter becomes a batter-runner or there are runners on base.

SECTION 7. QUICK PITCH.

The pitcher shall not attempt a quick return of the ball before the batter has taken a position in the batter's box or when the batter is off balance as a result of a pitch.

EFFECT —Sections 1-7: Any infraction of Sections 1-7 is an illegal pitch. A ball shall be called on the batter. Runners are not advanced.

EXCEPTION: If a batter swings at or contacts any illegal pitch, it is nullified and all play stands.

SECTION 8. WARM-UP PITCHES.

At the beginning of each half inning, or when a pitcher relieves another, not more than one minute may be used to deliver not more than three warm-up pitches. Play shall be suspended during this time. For excessive warm-up pitches, a pitcher shall be penalized by awarding a ball to the batter for each pitch. This does not apply if the umpire delays the start of play due to substitution, conference, injuries, etc.

NOTE: A pitcher returning to pitch in the same half inning will not receive warm-up pitches.

SECTION 9. NO PITCH.

No pitch shall be declared when:

A. The pitcher pitches during the suspension of play.

B. The ball slips from the pitcher's hand during the windup or during the backswing.

C. No player, manager or coach shall call time, employ any other word or phrase, or commit any act while the ball is alive and in play for the obvious purpose of trying to make the pitcher commit an illegal pitch.

NOTE: A warning shall be issued to the offending team, and a repeat of this type act by any member of the team warned shall result in the offender being removed from the game.

EFFECT - Section 9 A-C:

The ball is dead, and all subsequent action on that pitch is canceled.

RULE 7 - BATTING

SECTION 1. ON-DECK BATTER.

A. The on-deck batter is the offensive player whose name follows the name of the batter in the batting order.

B. The on-deck batter shall take a position within the lines of the on-deck circle nearest his bench.

C. The on-deck batter may loosen up with no more than two official softball bats, an approved warm-up bat, or a combination not to exceed two. Any detachable piece placed on the bat must be approved by the Equipment Standards Committee following a one-year period observed by members of this Committee.

D. The on-deck batter may leave the on-deck circle:
   1. When the on-deck batter becomes the batter.
   2. To direct runners advancing from third to home plate.

E. The on-deck batter may not interfere with the defensive player's opportunity to make an out:
   1. If it involves a runner, the runner closest to home plate at the time of the interference shall be declared out.
   2. If it is with the defensive fielder fielding a fly ball, the batter is out.

SECTION 2. BATTING ORDER.

A. The batting order of each team showing each player's first and last name, uniform number and position must be on the lineup card and must be delivered before the game by the manager or captain to the plate umpire. The plate umpire shall submit it to the inspection of the manager or captain of the opposing team.

B. The batting order delivered to the umpire must be followed throughout the game, unless a player is replaced by (a) a substitute who must take the place of the removed player in the batting order or (b) (Fast

Pitch Only) when the DEFO bats for the DP who will remain in the batting order spot until returning to the 10th spot in the lineup.

C. The first batter in each inning shall be the batter whose name follows that of the last player who completed his turn at bat in the preceding inning.

EFFECT - Section 2 B-C:

Except for a wrong batter at bat, batting out of order is an appeal play which may be made only by the defensive team. The defensive team forfeits its right to appeal batting out of order when one legal or illegal pitch has been made to the following batter, or when the pitcher and all infielders have clearly vacated their normal fielding positions and have left fair territory on their way to the bench or dugout.

　1. If the error is discovered while the incorrect batter is at bat, the correct batter may take the batter's position and legally assume any balls and strikes. Any runs scored or bases run while the incorrect batter was at bat shall be legal.
　　NOTE: The offensive team may correct a wrong batter at the plate with no penalty.

　2. If the error is discovered after the incorrect batter has completed a turn at bat and before a legal or illegal pitch has been made to the following batter or before the pitcher and all infielders have clearly vacated their normal fielding positions and have left fair territory on their way to the bench or dugout area: (a) the player who should have batted is out. (b) Any advance or score made because of a ball batted by the improper batter or because of the improper batter's advance to first base as a result of obstruction, an error, a hit batter, walk, dropped third strike or a base hit shall be

nullified. (c) The next batter is the player whose name follows that of the player called out for failing to bat. (d) If the batter declared out under these circumstances is the third out, the correct batter in the next inning shall be the player who would have come to bat had the player been put out by ordinary play.

3. If the error is discovered after the first legal or illegal pitch to the next batter, or after the pitcher and all infielders have clearly vacated their normal fielding positions and have left fair territory on their way to the bench or dugout area, the turn at bat of the incorrect batter is legal, all runs scored and ⁓es run are legal and the next batter in order shall be the one whose name follows that of the incorrect batter. No one is called out for failure to bat. Players who have not batted and who have not been called out have lost their turn at bat until reached again in the regular order.

4. No runner shall be removed from the base occupied except the batter-runner who has been taken off the base by the umpire as in (2) above to bat in his proper place. The correct batter merely misses the turn at bat with no penalty. The batter following the correct batter in the batting order becomes the legal batter.

D. The batting order for coed shall alternate the sexes. Coed play will use an 11-inch red-stitch ball when the female bats and a 12-inch red stitch ball when the male bats.

E. When the third out in an inning is made before the batter has completed his turn at bat, this player shall be the first batter in the next inning and the ball and strike count shall be canceled.

SECTION 3. BATTING POSITION.

A. The batter must have both feet completely within the lines of the batter's box prior to the start of the pitch. The batter may touch the lines, but no part of a foot may be outside the lines prior to the pitch.

B. The batter must take the batter's position within 10 seconds after being directed by the umpire. EFFECT: The umpire will call a strike. No pitch has to be thrown and the ball is dead.

C. (Junior Olympic Only) After entering the batter's box, the batter must remain in the box with at least one foot between pitches and while taking signals and practice swings.

EXCEPTIONS: The batter can leave the box (a) if the ball is hit fair or foul, (b) on the swing, slap or check swing, (c) if forced out of the box by a pitch, (d) on a wild pitch or passed ball, (e) if there is an attempted play, (f) if time out has been called, (g) if the pitcher leaves the eight-foot circle or the catcher leaves the catcher's, or (h) on a three ball pitch that is a strike which the batter thinks is a ball.

EFFECT: If the batter leaves the box illegally the umpire may warn the batter or call a strike.

NOTE: Any number of warnings and called strikes can be made with each batter. No pitch has to be thrown and the ball is dead.

D. The batter shall not step directly in front of the catcher to the other batter's box while the pitcher (FP Only) is taking the signal or (SP Only)is in position to pitch, or any time thereafter prior to the release of the pitch.

EFFECT: The ball is dead, the batter is out and the runners may not advance.

SECTION 4. A STRIKE IS CALLED BY THE UMPIRE.

A. (Fast Pitch Only) For each legally pitched ball entering the strike zone.

EFFECT: The ball is in play and the runners may advance with liability to be put out.

(Slow Pitch Only) For each legally pitched ball entering the strike zone before touching the ground and the batter does not swing. It is not a strike if the pitched ball touches home plate and then is swung at by the batter. Any pitched ball that hits the ground or plate cannot be legally swung at by the batter.

NOTE: If the batter swings and misses the pitch prior to the ball hitting the ground or plate, it is a strike.

EFFECT: The ball is dead.

B. For each legally pitched ball swung at and missed by the batter.

FAST PITCH EFFECT: The ball is in play and the runners may advance with liability to be put out.

SLOW PITCH EFFECT: The ball is dead. If the batter swings at an illegal pitch, the illegal pitch is nullified.

C. For each foul tip.

EFFECT: (Fast Pitch Only) The ball is in play and runners may advance with liability to be put out. The batter is out if it is the third strike.

(Slow Pitch Only) The ball is dead and the batter is out if it is the third strike.

(16-Inch Slow Pitch) The ball remains live; runners cannot advance.

D. (Fast Pitch Only) For each foul ball when the batter has fewer than two strikes.

E. (Slow Pitch Only) For each foul ball, including the third strike.

NOTE: A caught fly ball is not a foul ball.

F. For each pitched ball swung at and missed which touches any part of the batter.

G. When any part of the batter's person or clothing is hit with a batted ball when the batter is in the batter's box and (FP Only) has fewer than two strikes.

H. When a delivered ball by the pitcher hits the batter
while the ball is in the strike zone.

I. If the batter does not take the batter's position within
10 seconds after being directed by the umpire.

J. (Junior Olympics Only) When, between pitches, the
batter leaves the batter's box illegally or does not
return to the box after a warning.

EFFECT - Section 4 D-J:

The ball is dead and each runner must return to his
base without liability to be put out.

SECTION 5. A BALL IS CALLED BY THE UMPIRE.

A. (Fast Pitch Only) For each legally pitched ball which
does not enter the strike zone, touches the ground
before reaching home plate, or touches home plate,
and the batter does not swing.

EFFECT: The ball is in play and runners are entitled
to advance with liability to be put out.

(Slow Pitch Only) For each legally pitched ball which
does not enter the strike zone, touches the ground
before reaching home plate, or touches home plate,
and the batter does not swing. Any pitched ball that
hits the ground or plate cannot be legally swung at by
the batter. NOTE: If the batter swings at a pitch after
the ball hits the ground or plate, it is a ball. EFFECT:
The ball is dead and runners may not advance.

(16-Inch Slow Pitch): The ball remains live; however,
runners cannot advance.

B. (Fast Pitch Only) For each illegally pitched ball not
swung at.

EFFECT: The ball is dead and runners are entitled to
advance one base without liability to be put out.

EXCEPTION: Unless the offensive manager elects to
take the result of the play.

(Slow Pitch Only) For each illegally pitched ball not
swung at.

EFFECT: The ball is dead and runners may not advance.

C. (Slow Pitch Only) When a pitched ball hits the batter outside the strike zone.

D. When the catcher fails to return the ball directly to the pitcher as required.

E. For each excessive warm-up pitch.

EFFECT - Section 5 C-E:
The ball is dead and runners may not advance.

SECTION 6. THE BATTER IS OUT.

A. When the third strike is swung at, missed and the pitched ball touches any part of the batter's person.

B. When a batter enters the batter's box with or is discovered using an altered bat. The batter is also ejected from the game.

C. When the batter enters the batter's box with or is discovered using an illegal bat.

D. When an entire foot is touching the ground completely outside the lines of the batter's box when a fair or foul ball is hit.

E. When any part of a foot is touching home plate when a fair or foul ball is hit.

F. (Fast Pitch Only) When the batter bunts foul after the second strike. If the ball is caught in the air, it remains live and in play.

G. (Slow Pitch Only) When the batter bunts or chops the ball.

H. When members of the team at bat other than runners interfere with a player attempting to field a fly ball.

I. When the batter hits a fair ball with the bat a second time in fair territory.
EXCEPTION: If the batter is standing in the batter's box and contact is made while the bat is in the batter's hands, a foul ball is ruled even if the ball is hit a second time over fair territory.

NOTE: If the batter drops the bat and the ball rolls against the bat in fair territory, and, in the umpire's judgment, there was no intention to interfere with the course of the ball, the batter is not out and the ball is live and in play.

EFFECT - Section 6 A-I: The ball is dead and each runner must return to the base legally held at the time of the pitch.

J. (Slow Pitch Only) After a third strike, including a foul ball that is hit after two strikes.

   EXCEPTION: If a fly ball is caught **in playable territory**, the ball remains live.

K. When a called or swinging third strike is caught by the catcher.

L. (Fast Pitch Only) When the batter has three strikes if there are fewer than two outs and first base is occupied.

   EXCEPTION: (In Junior Olympic 10-Under the ball becomes dead and the batter is out.)

M. Whenever the batter due up has left the game under the Short-handed Rule. (See Rule 4, Section 1D.)

N. The batter shall not hinder the catcher from catching or throwing the ball by stepping out of the batter's box, or intentionally hinder the catcher while standing within the batter's box, **when the catcher is attampting to make a play on a runner(s);** or intefere with a play at home plate.

   EFFECT: The ball is dead, the batter is out and each runner must return to the last base that, in the judgment of the umpire, was touched at the time of the interference. **If no play is being made and the batter accidentally interferes with the catcher's return throw to the pitcher and a runner(s) advances safely, the umpire should call time and return the runner(s) to the base occupied at the time of the accidental interference.**

RULE 8 - BATTER-RUNNER AND RUNNER

SECTION 1.

THE BATTER BECOMES A BATTER-RUNNER.

A. As soon as he legally hits a fair ball.

B. (Fast Pitch Only) When the catcher fails to catch the third strike before the ball touches the ground when there are fewer than two outs and first base is unoccupied, or anytime there are two outs. This is called the third strike rule.

   EXCEPTION: (Junior Olympic 10-Under) The ball is dead and the batter is out.

   EFFECT - Section 1 A-B:

   The ball is in play, and the batter becomes a batter-runner with liability to be put out.

C. When four balls have been called by the umpire. The batter-runner is awarded one base without liability to be put out.

   EFFECT:

   1. (Fast Pitch Only) The ball is in play unless it has been blocked.

   2. (Slow Pitch Only) The ball is dead and runners may not advance unless forced. If the pitcher desires to walk a batter intentionally, he may do so by notifying the plate umpire who shall award the batter first base. If two batters are to be walked intentionally, the second intentional walk may not be administered until the first batter reaches first base.

      NOTE: If the umpire mistakenly allows two walks at one time and the first batter fails to touch first base, no appeal will be honored on the first batter.

   3. (Coed) The ball is dead. Any walk to a male batter will result in a two base award for the

batter. Runners are advanced only if forced to advance. The next batter (a female) will bat.
Exception: With two outs, the female batter has the option to walk or bat.
NOTE: Should the female batter-runner pass a male batter-runner when choosing to walk, no out shall be called during this dead ball period. A male batter-runner advancing to second without touching first base shall be called out if properly appealed.

D. When the catcher obstructs, hinders or prevents the batter from striking or hitting a pitched ball.
EFFECT:
   1. The umpire shall give a delayed dead ball signal.
   2. If the batter hits the ball and reaches first base safely, and if all other runners have advanced at least one base on the batted ball, catcher obstruction is canceled. All action as a result of the batted ball stands. No option is given.
   NOTE: Once a runner has passed a base, the runner is considered to have reached that base (whether missing the base or not) and no option is given.
   3. Otherwise the manager has the option to take the result of the play, or have the obstruction enforced by awarding the batter first base and advancing all other runners only if forced.

E. When a fair batted ball strikes the person, attached equipment, or clothing of an umpire or a runner. If the runner is hit with a fair batted ball while touching a base, the runner is not out.
EFFECT:
   1. If, after touching a fielder (including the pitcher), the ball is in play.

---

2. If, after passing a fielder other than the pitcher, and no other infielder had a chance to make an out, the ball is in play.

3. If before passing a fielder without being touched, the ball is dead. If the runner is hit by the ball while off base, the runner is out and the batter-runner is entitled to first base without liability to be put out. Any runner not forced by the batter-runner must return to the base reached prior to the interference. When a fair ball touches a runner who is in contact with a base, the ball remains dead or live depending on the position of the fielder closest to the base.

4. If the fair batted ball hits an umpire before passing a fielder other than a pitcher, the ball is dead and the batter-runner is entitled to first base without liability to be put out.

F. (Fast Pitch Only) When a pitched ball not swung at nor called a strike touches any part of the batter's person or clothing while in the batter's box. It does not matter if the ball strikes the ground before hitting the batter. The batter's hands are not to be considered a part of the bat.

EFFECT: The ball is dead. The batter is entitled to one base without liability to be put out.

EXCEPTION: If no attempt is made to avoid being hit, the batter will not be awarded first base unless it is ball four.

NOTE: **If the batter is hit on the hands while swinging at a pitch and hits the ball fair or foul, the ball is dead and a strike called. If it is strike three, the batter is out.**

SECTION 2. BATTER-RUNNER IS OUT.

A. (Fast Pitch Only) When the catcher drops the third

strike and is legally put out prior to reaching first base with less than two outs and first base not occupied.

B. When after hitting a fair ball he is legally put out prior to reaching first base.

C. When, after a fly ball is hit, the ball is caught by a fielder before it touches the ground, any object or person other than a defensive player.

EFFECT - Section 2 A-C:

The ball is in play.

D. When the batter-runner fails to advance to first base and enters the team area after a batted fair ball, a base on balls, a dropped third strike (Fast Pitch Only), or catcher obstruction.

EXCEPTION: In slow pitch on a base on balls, or on a hit batter (Fast Pitch Only) the ball is dead, the batter-runner is not out and runners cannot advance unless forced.

E. When he runs outside the three-foot (0.91m) lane and, in the judgment of the umpire, interferes with the fielder taking the throw at first base; however, the batter-runner may run outside the three-foot (0.91m) lane to avoid a fielder attempting to field a batted ball.

F. When the batter-runner interferes with a fielder attempting to field a batted ball, interferes with a fielder attempting to throw the ball, intentionally interferes with a thrown ball while out of the batter's box, makes contact with a fair batted ball before reaching first base, or (Fast Pitch Only) interferes with a dropped third strike. If this interference, in the umpire's judgment, is an obvious attempt to prevent a double play, the runner closest to home plate shall be called out.

NOTE: A batter-runner being hit with a thrown ball does not necessarily constitute interference.

G. When the batter-runner interferes with a play at home plate in an attempt to prevent an obvious out at home plate. The runner is also out.

H. When the batter-runner moves back toward home plate to avoid or delay a tag by a fielder.

EFFECT - Section 2 E-H:
The ball is dead and runner(s) must return to the last base legally touched at the time of interference.

I. When an infield fly is declared.

J. When an infielder intentionally drops a fair fly ball, including a line drive or a bunt, which can be caught with ordinary effort with first; first and second; first and third; or first, second and third bases occupied with fewer than two outs. A trapped ball shall not be considered as having been intentionally dropped.
EFFECT: The ball is dead, and each runner must return to the last base touched at the time of the pitch.
NOTE: If an infield fly is ruled, it has precedence over an intentionally dropped ball.

K. When the immediate preceding runner who is not yet out intentionally interferes, in the umpire's judgment, with a fielder who is attempting to catch a thrown ball or throw a ball in an attempt to complete the play on the batter-runner.
EFFECT: Batter-runner is out. The runner shall also be called out.

L. (Slow Pitch Only) For excess over-the-fence home runs.

M. If, when using the double base, there is a play on the batter-runner, the batter-runner touches only the white portion and the defense appeals prior to the batter-runner returning to first base.
Note: This is treated the same as missing the base.

N. If a spectator reaches into the field of play and interferes with a fielder's opportunity to catch a fly ball, the batter is out. **The umpires shall award the base or bases that in their judgment the runner(s) would have retouched had there been no interference.**

SECTION 3. TOUCHING BASES IN LEGAL ORDER.

A. When a runner must return to a base while the ball is in play or dead, the runner must touch the base(s) in reverse order. EXCEPTION: On a foul ball.

B. When a runner or batter-runner acquires the right to a base by touching it before being put out, the runner or batter-runner is entitled to hold the base until legally touching the next base in order or is forced to vacate it for a succeeding runner. NOTE: **When a runner passes a base, he is considered to have touched the base. This also applies to awarded bases.**

C. When a runner dislodges a base from its proper position, neither the runner nor the succeeding runner(s) in the same series of plays are compelled to follow a base out of position.

EFFECT - Section 3 B-C:

The ball is in play and runners may advance or return with liability to be put out.

D. A runner shall not run bases in reverse order either to confuse the fielders or to make a travesty of the game. EFFECT: The ball is dead and the runner is out.

E. Two runners may not occupy the same base simultaneously.

EFFECT: The runner who first legally occupied the base shall be entitled to it, unless forced to advance. The other runner may be put out by being touched with the ball.

F. Failure of a PRECEDING runner to touch a base or to legally tag up on a caught fly ball, and who is declared out, does not affect the status of a SUCCEEDING runner who touches bases in proper order. If the failure to touch a base in regular order or to legally tag up on a caught fly ball is the third out of the inning, no SUCCEEDING runner may score a run.

G. No runner may return to touch a missed base or one he had left too soon after a following runner has scored or once he leaves the field of play.

H. Bases left too soon on a caught fly ball must be retouched prior to advancing to awarded bases.

I. Awarded bases must be touched in legal order. EXCEPTION: (Super Slow Pitch Only **and all Men's Major Divisions of Slow Pitch**) On any fair batted ball hit over the fence for a home run, the batter and all runners are credited with a score. The batter and any runners on base do not need to run the bases. Note: This would eliminate any runner appeal play.

SECTION 4. RUNNERS ARE ENTITLED TO ADVANCE WITH LIABILITY TO BE PUT OUT.

A. (Fast Pitch Only) When the ball leaves the pitcher's hand on the delivery.

B. (Slow Pitch Only) When a pitched ball is batted or reaches home plate.

C. On a thrown ball or a fair batted ball that is not blocked.

D. On a thrown ball that hits an umpire.

E. When a legally caught fly ball is first touched.

F. If a fair ball strikes an umpire or a runner after having passed an infielder other than the pitcher, and provided no other infielder had a chance to make an out, or when a fair batted ball has been touched by an infielder, including the pitcher.

EFFECT - Section 4 A-F:
   The ball is in play.

G. (Super Slow Pitch and Men's Major Slow Pitch) Runners may advance when the ball reaches home plate **or**

if the pitcher has the ball and is not in the vicinity of the pitching plate.

NOTE: 1) If a runner stops while off the base, when the ball is returned to the pitcher, or the pitcher is about to receive the ball in the vicitinity of the pitcher's plate, the play is ruled dead and all runners are returned to the last base legally touched. **2) Runners may not advance if the pitch hits the batter, the ground before home plate, or home plate. Umpires will call a ball and give a dead ball signal when this occurs. 3) A runner may steal or advance on an illegal pitch. If thrown out, the runner will remain out.** 4)The pitcher may cover any base on an attempted put out and if a play is being made on a runner off the base, the ball remains live.

H. (10-Under Fast Pitch Only) Runners starting at first or second base are entitled to steal one base only per pitch with liability to be put out. Runners starting at third base may not steal or advance home, but are liable to be put out if they come off the base.

NOTE: 1) A runner, attempting to advance beyond the one base they are entitled to steal, may be put out while between bases. A runner cannot be put out while in sole contact with a base. 2) After all play ceases, and the ball becomes dead, if a runner occupies a base beyond the one the runner was entitled to steal, the runner will be returned to the correct base without liability to be put out.

SECTION 5. A RUNNER FORFEITS HIS EXEMPTION FROM LIABILITY TO BE PUT OUT.

A. If, while the ball is in play or on awarded bases, the runner fails to touch a base before attempting to make the next base.

B. If, after overrunning first base, the runner attempts to continue to second base.

C. If, after dislodging a base, a runner attempts to continue to the next base.

D. (16-Inch Slow Pitch Only) A runner may lead off any base with the risk of being picked off by a throw from the pitcher or catcher. If a throw results in an overthrown or blocked ball, no runners may advance. Any runner advancing on a pitch not hit is liable to be put out if tagged before returning to his original base.

SECTION 6. RUNNERS ARE ENTITLED TO ADVANCE WITHOUT LIABILITY TO BE PUT OUT.

A. When forced to vacate a base because the batter was awarded a base on balls.
EFFECT: (Fast Pitch Only) The ball remains in play unless it is blocked. Any runner affected is entitled to one base and may advance farther at their own risk if the ball is in play. (Slow Pitch Only) The ball is dead.

B. When a fielder not in possession of the ball, not in the act of fielding a batted ball, or not about to receive a thrown ball, impedes the progress of a runner or batter-runner who is legally running bases.
NOTE: Obstructed runners are still required to touch all bases in proper order, or they could be called out on a proper appeal by the defensive team. Should an act of interference occur following any obstruction, enforcement of the interference penalty would have precedence.

1. If the obstructed runner is put out prior to reaching the base which would have been reached had there not been obstruction, a dead ball is called and the obstructed runner and each other runner affected by the obstruction

will always be awarded the base or bases which would have been reached, in the umpire's judgment, had there not been obstruction. An obstructed runner may not be called out between the two bases where obstructed unless properly appealed for missing a base, leaving a base before a fly ball was first touched, for an act of interference, or if passing another runner.

2. If the obstructed runner is put out after passing the base he would have reached had there not been obstruction, the obstructed runner will be called out. The ball remains live.

3. When a runner, while advancing or returning to a base, is obstructed by a fielder who neither has the ball nor is attempting to field a batted or thrown ball, or a fielder who fakes a tag without the ball, the obstructed runner and each other runner affected by the obstruction will always be awarded the base or bases which would have been reached, in the umpire's judgment, had there been no obstruction. If the umpire feels there is justification, a defensive player making a fake tag could be ejected from the game.

4. Catcher obstruction on the batter is covered under Rule 8, Section 1D.
   EFFECT: When any obstruction occurs (including a rundown), the umpire will signal a delayed dead ball. The ball will remain alive.

C. (Fast Pitch Only) When a wild pitch or passed ball lodges in or goes under, over or through the backstop.
   EFFECT: The ball is dead and all runners are awarded one base only. The batter is awarded first base only on the fourth ball.

D. When forced to vacate a base because the batter was awarded first base.

E. (Fast Pitch Only) When a pitcher makes an illegal pitch, providing the offensive coach does not take the result of the play.

F. When a fielder intentionally contacts or catches a fair batted or thrown ball with his cap, helmet, mask, protector, pocket, detached glove or any part of his uniform which is detached from its proper place on his person.

EFFECT: The runners would be entitled to three bases from the time of the pitch if a batted ball, or two bases from the time of the throw if a thrown ball, and in either case, they may advance farther at their own risk. If the illegal catch or touch is made on a fair hit ball which, in the judgment of the umpire, would have cleared the outfield fence in flight, the batter-runner shall be awarded a four base award.

G. When the ball is in play and is overthrown (beyond the boundary lines) or is blocked.

EFFECT: All runners will be awarded two bases, and the award will be governed by the positions of the runners when the ball left the fielder's hand. Runners may return to touch a missed base or base left too soon. If two runners are between the same bases, the award is based on the position of the lead runner.

EXCEPTION:

1. When a fielder loses possession of the ball, such as on an attempted tag, and the ball enters the dead ball area or becomes blocked, each runner is awarded one base from the last base touched at the time the ball entered the dead ball area or became blocked.

2. **When the ball becomes dead, no runner may return to touch a missed base or a base left too**

soon if he has advanced, touched, and remains a base beyond the missed base or the base left too soon.

3. If the ball becomes blocked due to offensive equipment not involved in the game, the ball is ruled dead and runners are returned to the last base touched at the time of the blocked ball. If the blocked ball prevented the defense from making an out, the runner being played on is called out.

4. If an awarded base is in error, after one pitch is thrown (legal or illegal), the error cannot be corrected.

H. When a fair batted fly ball strikes the foul pole above the fence level or leaves the playing field in fair territory without touching the ground or going through the fence. It shall entitle the batter-runner to a home run, unless it passes out of the grounds at a distance less than the prescribed fence distances from home plate, in which case the batter-runner would be entitled to only two bases.

I. When a fair ball bounces over or rolls under or through a fence or any designated boundary of the playing field. Also, when it deflects off of a defensive player and goes out of play in foul territory, deflects off a runner or umpire after having passed an infielder excluding the pitcher and provided **no other fielder** had a chance to make an out.

EFFECT: The ball is dead, and all runners are awarded two bases from the time of the pitch.

J. When a live ball is unintentionally carried by a fielder from playable territory into dead ball territory.

EFFECT: The ball is dead and each runner is awarded one base from the last base touched at the time the fielder entered dead ball territory.

NOTE: A fielder carrying a live ball into the dugout or team area to tag a player is considered to have unintentionally carried it there.

K. If, in the judgment of the umpire, a fielder intentionally carries, kicks, pushes or throws a live ball from playable territory into dead ball territory.

EFFECT: The ball is dead. Each runner is awarded two bases from the last base touched at the time the fielder entered or the ball was kicked, pushed or thrown into dead ball territory.

L. When there is spectator interference with any thrown or fair batted ball, the ball is dead at the moment of interference and the umpire shall award the base or bases that in his judgment the runner(s) would have reached had there not been interference.

SECTION 7. A RUNNER MUST RETURN TO HIS BASE.

A. When a batted ball is foul.

B. When an illegally batted ball is declared by the umpire. **NOTE: Prior to a pitch (legal or illegal) to the next batter, if the runner was discovered having used an illegal bat, he shall be declared out. If the bat was altered, he shall also be ejected. In either case, if the altered/illegal bat is discovered prior to the next pitch, any advance by runners shall be nullified.**

C. When a batter, batter-runner or runner is called out for interference. Each other runner shall return to the last base which, in the umpire's judgment, was legally touched by the runner at the time of the interference.

D. (Fast Pitch Only) When any part of the batter's person or clothing is touched by a pitched ball that is swung at and missed.

E. (Fast Pitch Only) When a batter is hit by a pitched ball, unless forced.

EFFECT - Section 7 A-E:

1. The ball is dead.
2. Each runner must return to his base without liability to be put out, except when forced to go to the next base because the batter became a batter-runner.
3. Runners need not touch the intervening bases in returning to their base.

F. (Fast Pitch Only) When the plate umpire or any part of his clothing interferes with the catcher's attempt to throw out a runner stealing, or an attempted pick off play.

EFFECT: This is a delayed dead ball at the time of the interference. If the runner is ruled out, the ball remains live. If the runner is not out, return him to the base occupied at the start of the pitch.

Note: It is not umpire interference if, on a passed ball or wild pitch, the umpire gets hit by a thrown ball from the catcher. The ball is live.

G. (Slow Pitch Only) Base stealing is not allowed.

EFFECT: Each runner may leave a base when a pitched ball is batted, touches the ground or reaches home, but must return to that base immediately after each pitch not hit by the batter.

EXCEPTION: (16-Inch Slow Pitch Only) Runners may lead off prior to a pitched ball. **(Super Slow Pitch and Men's Major Slow Pitch Only)** Runners may advance after the ball reaches home plate.

H. When an intentionally dropped ball is ruled.

SECTION 8. THE RUNNER IS OUT.

A. When running to any base in regular or reverse order and the runner runs more than three feet (0.91 m) from the base path to avoid being touched by the ball in the hand(s) of a fielder.

B. When the ball is in play and while the runner is not in contact with a base, the runner is legally touched with the ball in the hand(s) of a fielder.

C. When, on a force play, a fielder contacts the base while holding the ball, touches the ball to the base or tags the runner before the runner reaches the base.

D. When the runner physically passes a preceding runner before that runner has been put out.
NOTE: If this was the third out of the inning, any runs scoring prior to the out for passing a preceding runner would count.

E. When anyone other than another runner physically assists the runner while the ball is in play.

EFFECT - Section 8 A-E:
The ball is in play and the runner is out.

F. When the runner leaves a base to advance to another base before a caught fly ball has touched a fielder, provided the ball is returned to an infielder and properly appealed.

G. When the runner fails to touch the intervening base or bases in regular or reverse order and the ball is returned to an infielder and properly appealed. If the runner put out is the batter-runner at first base, or any other runner forced to advance because the batter became a batter-runner, this is a force out.

H. When the batter-runner legally overruns first base, attempts to run to second base and is legally touched while off base.

I. When running or sliding for home plate and the runner fails to touch it, and a fielder properly appeals to the umpire for the decision.

EFFECT Section 8 F-I:

1. These are appeal plays, and the defensive team loses the privilege of putting the runner out if: (a) the appeal is not made before the next legal or illegal pitch, (b) the pitcher and all infielders have clearly vacated their normal fielding positions and have left fair territory on their way to the bench or dugout area, or (c) on the last play of the game, the umpires have left the field of play.

2. (Live Ball Appeal) If properly appealed during a live ball, the runner is out. (POE # 1 B)

3. (Dead Ball Appeal) Once the ball has been returned to the infield and time has been called, any infielder (including the pitcher or catcher), with or without possession of the ball, may make a verbal appeal on a runner missing a base or leaving a base too soon on a caught fly ball. The administering umpire should acknowledge the appeal and then make a decision on the play. No runner may leave his base during this period as the ball remains dead until the next pitch. NOTE:

   (a) If the ball goes out of play, the dead ball appeal cannot be made until the completion of all legal advancement of all base runners.

   (b) If the pitcher has possession of the ball and is in contact with the pitching plate when making a verbal appeal, no illegal pitch is called.

   (c) If "play ball" has been declared by the umpire and the pitcher then requests an appeal, the umpire would again call "time" and allow the appeal process.

J. When the runner interferes with a fielder attempting to field a batted ball, interferes with a fielder attempting to throw the ball or intentionally interferes with a thrown ball. If this interference, in the judgment of the umpire, is an obvious attempt to prevent a double play and occurs before the runner is put out, the immediate succeeding runner shall also be called out.

NOTE: If a ball ricochets off one defensive player and another player has the opportunity to make an out, the runner will be ruled out if he interferes with the second fielder.

K. When the runner is struck with a fair untouched batted ball while not in contact with a base and before it passes an infielder, excluding the pitcher, or if it passes an infielder and **any defensive player** has an opportunity to make an out.

L. When a runner intentionally kicks a fair ball which an infielder has missed.

NOTE - Section 8 J-L:

When runners are called out for interference, the batter-runner is awarded first base and credited with a base hit. **Runners are advanced only if forced by the batter-runner being awarded first base.**

EXCEPTION: If interference occurs by the runner on a foul fly ball not caught, the runner is out, the ball is dead, a strike is called, and the batter remains at bat. (Slow Pitch Only) If this is the third strike, it would be two outs.

M. When the coach near third base runs in the direction of home plate on or near the baseline while a fielder is attempting to make a play on a batted or thrown ball and thereby draws a throw to home plate. The runner closest to home shall be declared out.

N. When one or more members of the offensive team stand or collect around a base to which a runner is advancing, thereby confusing the fielders and adding to the difficulty of making the play.

NOTE: Members of a team include bat boy or any other person authorized to sit on the team's bench.

O. When a coach intentionally interferes with a thrown ball while in the coach's box, or interferes with the defensive team's opportunity to make a play on another runner. The runner closest to home plate at the time of the interference shall be declared out.

P. When, after being declared out or after scoring, a runner interferes with a defensive player's opportunity to make a play on another runner. The runner closest to home plate at the time of the interference shall be declared out.

NOTE: A runner continuing to run and drawing a throw will be considered a form of interference. This does not apply **to batter-runner** running on the **third strike rule.**

Q. When a defensive player has the ball, or is about to catch a thrown ball, and the runner remains on his feet and crashes into the defensive player.

NOTE: If the act is determined to be flagrant, the offender shall be ejected. An errant throw drawing the defense into the path of the runner is not interference.

EFFECT - Section 8 J-Q: The ball is dead and the runner is out. Each other runner must return to the last base legally touched at the time of the interference.

R. (Slow Pitch Only) When a runner fails to keep contact with the base to which they are entitled until a pitched ball touches the ground, reaches home plate or is batted.

EXCEPTION: (16-Inch Slow Pitch Only) Any runner may leave a base as soon as the ball is declared in play.

S. (Fast Pitch Only) When a runner fails to keep contact with the base to which a runner is entitled until the ball leaves the pitcher's hand.

T. (Fast Pitch Only) When a runner is legitimately off a base after a pitch or as a result of a batter completing a turn at bat, and while the pitcher has the ball within an eight foot (2.44m) radius of the pitcher's plate, the runner must immediately return to the base or attempt to advance to the next base.

  1. Failure to immediately return non-stop to the base or proceed non-stop to the next base will result in the runner being declared out.

  2. Once the runner stops at a base for any reason, he will be declared out if he leaves the base. EXCEPTION: The runner will not be declared out if a play is made on him or another runner (a fake throw is considered a play), the pitcher no longer has possession of the ball within the eight foot (2.44 m) radius, or the pitcher releases the ball on a pitch to the batter. NOTE: A base on balls or dropped third strike on which any runner is entitled to run past any base is treated the same as a batted ball. The batter-runner may continue past any base and is entitled to run as long as he does not stop. If he stops after he rounds any base, he then must comply with (1) above.

EFFECT: Section R-T:

  The ball is dead, "no pitch" is declared when applicable and the runner is out.

  NOTE: If two runners or more runners are off their bases, when one is called out, the ball is dead and other runners are returned to the last base touched. Only one runner may be called out.

U. When he abandons a base and enters his team area or leaves the field of play.

V. When he positions himself behind and not in contact with a base to get a running start on any fly ball. The ball remains alive.

W. Whenever a runner on base leaves the game under the shorthanded rule. (Rule 4, Section 1D)

X. (Senior SP Only) When as a courtesy runner on base, it is their turn to bat.

SECTION 9. RUNNER IS NOT OUT.

A. When a runner runs behind or in front of the fielder and outside the base line in order to avoid interfering with a fielder attempting to field the ball in the base path.

B. When the runner does not run in a direct line to a base, provided the fielder in the direct line does not have the ball in possession.

C. When more than one fielder attempts to field a batted ball and the runner comes into contact with the one who, in the judgment of the umpire, could not have made an out.

D. When a runner is hit with a fair, untouched batted ball that has passed an infielder, excluding the pitcher, and, in the judgment of the umpire, **no other fielder** had a chance to make an out.

E. When a runner is hit with a fair, untouched batted ball over foul territory that, in the judgment of the umpire, **no fielder** had a chance to make an out.

F. When a runner is hit by a fair batted ball after it touches, or is touched by, any fielder, including the pitcher, and the runner could not avoid contact with the ball.

G. When a runner is touched while off base:

1. With a ball not securely held by a fielder.

     2. With a hand or glove of a defensive player and the ball is in the other hand.

H. When the defensive team does not request the umpire's decision on an appeal play until after the next legal or illegal pitch, or until after the pitcher and all infielders have clearly vacated their normal fielding positions and have left fair territory on their way to the bench or dugout area, or after the last play of the game, the umpires have left the field of play.

I. When a batter-runner overruns first base after touching it and returns directly to the base.

J. When the runner is not given sufficient time to return to a base. The runner will not be called out for being off base before the pitcher releases the ball. "No pitch" will be called by the umpire.

K. When he has legally started to advance. The runner may not be stopped by the pitcher receiving the ball while on the pitching plate, nor by the pitcher stepping on the plate with the ball in his possession.

L. When the runner stays on the base until a fly ball touches the fielder and then attempts to advance.

M. When hit by a batted ball when touching the base, unless the runner intentionally interferes with the ball or a fielder making a play. (See Rule 8, Section 1 E (1-3).)

N. When the runner slides into a base and dislodges it from its proper position. The base is considered to have followed the runner.

EFFECT: A runner reaching a base safely will not be out for being off that base if it becomes dislodged. The runner may return without liability to be put out when the base has been replaced. A runner forfeits this exemption if they attempt to advance beyond the dislodged base before it is again in proper position.

O. When a fielder makes a play (**a pitch by the pitcher is not considered making a play**) on a batter, batter-runner or runner while using an illegal glove, and it is discovered before: a) the next pitch (legal or illegal); b) the pitcher and all infielders have left fair territory and the catcher has left his normal fielding position on the way to the dugout, or c) the umpires have left the field; the manager of the offended team is given one of two options:

1. The manager may have the entire play nullified with each runner returning to his original base and the batter batting over again, assuming the ball and strike count prior to the pitch that was hit.

2. The manager may take the result of the play and disregard the illegal act.

SECTION 10. RUNNING (Senior Men's Only).

A. Courtesy Runners. Unlimited courtesy runners are allowed each inning.

1. **Any player on the official lineup sheet including available substitutes may be used as a courtesy runner.**

2. A player may be a courtesy runner only once per inning.
   EFFECT: If a player runs the second time in the same inning, he will be called out and removed from the base.

3. A courtesy runner whose turn at bat comes while he is on base will be out. He will be removed from the base and come to bat. A second courtesy runner cannot be substituted at this time.

4. A courtesy runner may not run for an existing courtesy runner except for an injury.

   5. A courtesy runner is in the game when he touches the base.

B. Runners must touch the second home plate located adjacent to the right handed batter's box in order to be safe at home. Defensive players can only touch the original home plate and runners can only touch the second home plate. Runners tagged by the defensive team will not be out. If the runner touches the original home plate, he will be out and the ball will remain live. (See diagram under Rule 2, Section 3G)

C. Once a runner crosses a line 20 feet from home plate, he cannot return to third base.
   EFFECT: The runner will be called out if he returns and the ball remains live.

RULE 9 - PROTESTS

SECTION 1. Protests will not be received or considered if they are based solely on a decision involving the accuracy of judgment on the part of an umpire. Examples of protests which will not be considered are:

A. Whether a batted ball was fair or foul.

B. Whether a runner was safe or out.

C. Whether a pitched ball was a ball or a strike.

D. Whether a pitch was legal or illegal.

E. Whether a runner did or did not touch a base.

F. Whether a runner did or did not leave a base too soon on a caught fly ball.

G. Whether a fly ball was or was not caught legally.

H. Whether it was or was not an infield fly.

I. Whether there was or was not interference or obstruction.

J. Whether the field is or is not fit to continue or resume play.

K. Whether there is or is not sufficient light to continue play.

L. Whether a player or live ball did or did not enter a dead ball area or touch some object or person in a dead ball area.

M. Whether a batted ball did or did not clear the fence in flight.

N. Whether a batted ball was or was not touched by a fielder before clearing the fence in flight.

O. Any other matter involving only the accuracy of the umpire's judgment.

SECTION 2. PROTESTS. There are three types of protests:

A. Misinterpretation of a playing rule - must be made before the next pitch or, before all infielders have left fair territory, or if on the last play of the game, before the umpires leave the playing field.

NOTE: After one pitch has been thrown (legal or illegal) no change can be made on any umpire's ruling.

B. Illegal substitute or re-entry - must be made while they are in the game and before the umpires leave the playing field.

NOTE: An umpire cannot reverse a decision after a pitch (legal or illegal) to the next batter.

C. Ineligible player - can be made any time. Eligibility is the decision of the protest committee. (See ASA Code 201 A 7)

SECTION 3. Protests may involve both a matter of judgment and the interpretation of a rule.

EXAMPLE: With one out and runners on second and third, the batter flies out. The runner on third base tags up after the catch, but the runner on second does not. The runner on third crosses the plate before the ball is played at second base for the third out. The umpire does not allow the run to score. The questions as to whether the runners left their bases before the catch or whether the play at second base was made before the runner on third crossed the plate are solely matters of judgment and are not protestable. It is a misinterpretation of a playing rule and a proper subject for protest, however, if the umpire fails to allow the run to score.

SECTION 4.

A. The manager, acting manager or captain of the protesting team shall immediately notify the plate umpire that the game is being played under protest. The plate umpire shall in turn notify the opposing manager and official scorekeeper.

B. To aid in the correct determination of the issue, all interested parties shall take notice of the information, details and conditions surrounding the decision to protest.

SECTION 5. The official written protest must be filed within a reasonable time. In the absence of a league or tournament rule establishing the time limit for filing a protest, a protest should be considered if filed within a reasonable time, depending upon the nature of the call and the difficulty of obtaining the information relevant to the protest.

SECTION 6. The written protest should contain the following information:
A. The date, time and place of the game.
B. The names of the umpires and scorers.
C. The rule and section of the official rules or local rules under which the protest is made.
D. The information, details and conditions pertinent to the decision to protest.
E. All essential facts involved in the matter protested.

SECTION 7. The decision rendered on a protested game must result in one of the following:
A. The protest is considered to be invalid and the game score stands as played.
B. When a protest is determined to be valid because of the misinterpretation of a playing rule, the decision will be corrected and the game shall be replayed from the point at which the incorrect decision was made.
C. When a protest for ineligibility is determined to be valid, the offending team shall forfeit the game being played or the game last played to the offended team.

RULE 10 - UMPIRES

NOTE: Failure of umpires to adhere to Rule 10 shall not be grounds for protest. These are guidelines for umpires.

SECTION 1. POWER AND DUTIES.

The umpires are the representative of the league or organization by which they have been assigned to a particular game and, as such, are authorized and required to enforce each section of these rules. They have the power to order a player, coach, captain or manager to carry out or to omit any act which, in their judgment, is necessary to give force and effect to one or all of these rules, and to inflict penalties as herein prescribed, The plate umpire shall have the authority to make decisions on any situations not specifically covered in the rules. The following is the general information for umpires.

A. The umpire will not be a member of either team (i.e., player, coach, manager, officer, scorer or sponsor).

B. The umpire should be sure of the date, time, and place of the game and should arrive at the playing field 20 to 30 minutes ahead of time, start the game at the designated time, and leave the field when the game is over. The umpire's jurisdiction begins when entering the field to check the bats and ends when leaving the field following the completion of the game.

C. The male and female umpire shall wear a powder blue, short-sleeve shirt, dark navy blue socks and slacks and a cap with white with blue trim ASA letters on the front. The ball bag, jacket and/or sweater (all with the approved logo) must also be dark navy blue, and shoes and belt must be black for both male and female umpires. A T-shirt is optional to wear under the powder blue shirt; however, if one is worn, it must be white. The plate umpire in fast pitch MUST wear a black mask, black padding and black throat protector. (An extended wire protector may be worn in lieu of a throat protector on the mask.)

D. The umpires should introduce themselves to the captains, managers and scorers.

E. The umpires should inspect the playing field boundaries and equipment and clarify all ground rules for the representatives of both teams.

F. Each umpire will have the power to make decisions on violations committed during playing time or during suspension of play.

G. No umpire has the authority to set aside or question decisions made by another umpire within the limits of the respective duties as outlined in these rules.

H. An umpire may consult the other umpires at any time; however, the final decision will rest with the umpire whose exclusive authority it is to make the decision and who requests the opinion of the other umpire(s).

I. In order to define respective duties, the umpire whose primary responsibility is the judging of balls and strikes will be designated as the PLATE UMPIRE, while the umpire whose primary responsibility is the rendering of base decisions will be designated as the BASE UMPIRE.

J. The plate umpire and base umpire will have equal authority to:

　　1. Call a runner out for leaving a base too soon.
　　2. Call TIME for suspension of play.
　　3. Eject a player, coach, manager or other team member from the game for violation of rules or flagrant misconduct.
　　4. Call all illegal pitches.
　　5. Forfeit any game.

K. The umpire will declare the batter or runner out, without waiting for an appeal for such decision, in all cases where such player is retired in accordance with these rules.

NOTE: Unless appealed to, the umpire will not call a player out for failure to touch a base, for leaving a base too soon on a caught fly ball, for batting out of order, or for making an attempt to go to second after reaching first base, as provided in these rules.

L. The umpire will not penalize a team for any infraction of a rule when imposing the penalty would be to the advantage of the offending team.

SECTION 2. THE PLATE UMPIRE SHOULD.

A. Take a position behind the catcher. The plate umpire will have full charge of and be responsible for the proper conduct of the game.

B. Call balls and strikes, unless requesting the help of another umpire.

C. By agreement and in cooperation with the base umpire, make decisions on plays, fair or foul balls and legally or illegally caught balls. On plays which would necessitate the base umpire leaving the infield in a two umpire system, the plate umpire will assume the duties normally required of the base umpire.

D. Determine and declare whether:
    1. A batter bunts or chops a ball.
    2. A batted ball touches the person or clothing of the batter.
    3. A fly ball is an infield or an outfield fly.

E. Render base decisions as indicated in the Umpire's Manual.

F. Assume all duties when assigned as a single umpire to a game.

SECTION 3. THE BASE UMPIRE SHOULD.

A. Take such positions on the playing field as outlined in the Umpire's Manual.

B. Assist the plate umpire in every way to enforce the rules of the game.

SECTION 4. RESPONSIBILITIES OF A SINGLE UMPIRE.

If only one umpire is assigned, his duties and jurisdictions will extend to all points. The umpire's starting position for each pitch should be from behind home plate. On each batted ball or play that develops, the umpire must move out from behind the plate and into the infield to obtain the best position for any play that develops.

SECTION 5. CHANGE OF UMPIRES.

Teams may not request a change of umpires during a game unless an umpire is incapacitated by injury or illness.

SECTION 6. UMPIRE'S JUDGMENT.

A. There will be no appeal on any decision of any umpire on the grounds that the umpire was not correct in the conclusion as to whether a batted ball was fair or foul, a runner safe or out, a pitched ball is a ball or strike, or on any play involving accuracy of judgment. No decision rendered by any umpire will be reversed except when the umpire is convinced it is in violation of one of these rules. In case the manager, acting manager or captain of either team does seek reversal of a decision based solely on a point of rules, the umpire whose decision is in question will, if in doubt, confer with the umpire(s) before taking any action; but under no circumstances will any player or person, other than the manager, acting manager or captain of either team, have any legal right to protest any decision and seek its reversal on a claim that it is in conflict with these rules. **NOTE (Super Slow Pitch Only): Any arguing on the judgment of balls and strikes will constitute a team warning. Any repeat offense shall result in the ejection of that team member.**

B. Under no circumstances will any umpire seek to reverse a decision made by an associate, nor will any umpire criticize or interfere with the duties of his associate(s) unless asked to do so.

C. The umpire-in-chief may rectify any situation in which the reversal of an umpire's decision or a delayed call by an umpire places a batter-runner, a runner or the defensive team in jeopardy. This correction is not possible after one legal or illegal pitch has been thrown, or after the pitcher and all infielders have clearly vacated their normal fielding positions and have left fair territory on their way to the bench or dugout area, or after the last play of the game, the umpires have left the field of play.

SECTION 7. SIGNALS.

A. **Safe.** Body upright, eyes on the ball, and arms extended straight out with the palms down. A verbal call of "safe" is made as the arms are snapped to this position from the upper chest.

B. **Safe Sell**. The same as the safe call but as the arms are extended straight out with the palms down a step should be taken towards the play.

C. **Out.** Body upright, eyes on the ball and right arm extended straight up as an extension of the shoulder. As we come to the HAMMER position, the elbow is bent at a 90-degree angle and the fist closed with the fingers facing the right ear. The left arm should be brought to the midsection of the body. A verbal call of "out" is made as the right arm is extended high into the air and continued as the arm drops into the HAMMER position.

D. **Out Sell.** Come to upright position and take a step with left foot directly at the play. Your head should remain in position looking at the play as the upper torso turns perpendicularly from the play. Raise right arm with an open hand behind your head into a throwing position as you shuffle your right foot behind the left. Plant right foot and transfer weight, bringing right arm over the top of your head with a closed fist, and make a vigorous "out" call. Finish call by transferring your weight to the left foot while bringing the right foot forward and parallel to the left.

E. **Strike.** Body upright, eyes on the pitcher and right arm extended straight up as an extension of the shoulder. As we come to the HAMMER position, the elbow is bent at a 90-degree angle and the fist is closed with the fingers facing the right ear. The left arm should be brought to the midsection of the body. A verbal call of "strike" is made as the right arm is extended high into the air and continued as the arm drops into the HAMMER position.

F. **Fair Ball.** Body upright, eyes on the ball and point toward fair territory with the arm toward the infield. There is no verbal call on a fair ball, and if the umpire is wearing a mask, it should be in the left hand.

G. **Foul Ball.** On all foul balls, the ball is dead and the dead ball signal should be given. For balls touched close to the foul line over foul territory, the arms should be extended straight out from the shoulder toward foul territory away from the playing field. Follow with a dead ball signal. A verbal call of "foul ball" should be declared as the dead ball signal is given.

H. **Time Out/Dead Ball/No Pitch.** Body upright and both arms extended high into the air with the palms of the hands open and facing away from the umpire's body. A verbal call of "time out", "dead ball" or "no pitch" is made at the same time the arms are going up.

I. **Play Ball.** Body upright, eyes on the pitcher and the umpire makes a motion toward the pitcher. On a right-handed batter use the right hand. On a left-handed batter use the left hand. A verbal call of "play" or "play ball" is made as the umpire motions toward the pitcher.

J. **Hold Up Play.** Body upright and raise either hand with the palm facing the pitcher. On a right-handed batter use the right hand. On a left-handed batter use the left hand. "No pitch" shall be declared if the pitcher pitches while the umpire has a hand in this position.

K. **Delayed Dead Ball.** Body upright, the left arm is extended straight out to the side of the body as an extension of the shoulder and the left hand is in a fist. This position is held long enough for the players to see that the umpire has observed the act that caused this call.

L. **Infield Fly.** Body upright, eyes on the ball and right arm extended high into the air with a closed fist. Make a verbal call of "Infield Fly". If the batted ball is near a foul line, call "Infield Fly if Fair."

M. **Trapped Ball.** Same as safe signal. The umpire makes a verbal call of "safe."

N. **Foul Tip.** Body upright and eyes on the ball. The fingers of both hands are touched together and then the umpire gives the strike signal with no verbal call. This indicates that the bat tipped the ball and was caught by the catcher.

O. **Count.** Body upright. Have eye contact with the pitcher. Both hands are extended high above the head.

Consecutive fingers are used to indicate the ball and strike count on the batter. Use the fingers of the left hand for balls and the fingers of the right hand for strikes. A verbal description of the count on the batter is given while the hands are overhead. Balls are always mentioned first and strikes second.

P. **Double.** Body upright. Raise the right hand high above the head indicating with two fingers the number of bases awarded. A verbal call of "two bases" is made while the hand remains overhead.

Q. **Home Run.** Body upright. Raise the right hand high above the head with a closed fist. Make a counter-clockwise circling motion with the raised fist. A verbal call of "home run" is made at the same time the fist is overhead.

R. **Four-Base Award.** Body upright. Raise the right hand high above the head with four fingers shown. A verbal call of "four-base award" is made at the same time the hand is overhead.

SECTION 8. SUSPENSION OF PLAY.

A. Umpires may suspend play when, in their judgment, conditions justify such action.

B. Play will be suspended whenever the plate umpire leaves the umpire's position to brush the plate or to perform other duties not directly connected with the calling of plays.

C. The umpire will suspend play whenever a batter or pitcher steps out of position for a legitimate reason.

D. An umpire will suspend play if a fair batted ball hits the umpire prior to passing an infielder.
EFFECT: The batter-runner is awarded a base hit. No runners are advanced unless forced to advance.

E. An umpire will not call time while any play is in progress, including when a thrown ball hits an umpire.

F. An umpire will not call time after the pitcher has started his delivery.

G. In case of injury, time will not be called until all plays in progress have been completed or each runner has been held at his base.

H. Umpires will not suspend play at the request of players, coaches or managers until all action in progress has been completed.

I. (Slow Pitch Only) When, in the judgment of an umpire, all immediate play is apparently completed, the umpire should call time.

SECTION 9. VIOLATIONS AND PENALTIES.

A. Players, coaches, managers or other team members will not make disparaging or insulting remarks to or about opposing players, officials or spectators or commit other acts that could be considered unsportsmanlike conduct.

B. There will be no more than two coaches for each team to give words or signals of assistance and direction to the members of their team while at bat. One should be stationed near first base and the other near third base. Each coach must remain in his coach's box.

C. The penalty for violations by a player is prompt ejection of the offender from the game. For the first offense, a coach or manager may be warned, but for the second offense he is ejected from the game. The offender may remain on the bench. If the act is flagrant or if continued unsportsmanlike conduct comes from the ejected player on the bench, the offender should go directly to the dressing room or leave the grounds for the remainder of the game. Failure to do so will warrant a forfeiture of the game.

RULE 11 - SCORING

NOTE: Failure of official scorer to adhere to Rule 11 shall not be grounds for protest. These are guidelines for the official scorer.

SECTION 1. THE OFFICIAL SCORER SHALL KEEP RECORDS OF EACH GAME AS OUTLINED IN THE FOLLOWING RULES.

The official scorer shall have sole authority to make all decisions involving judgment. For example, it is the scorer's responsibility to determine whether a batter-runner's advance to first base is the result of a hit or an error; however, a scorer shall not make a decision which conflicts with the official playing rules or with an umpire's decision.

SECTION 2. THE BOX SCORE.

A. Each player's name and the position or positions played shall be listed in the order in which the player batted or would have batted had he not been removed or had the game not ended before the player's turn at bat.

1. (Fast Pitch Only) The designated player (DP) is optional, but if one is used, it must be made known prior to the start of the game and listed on the score sheet in the regular batting order. Ten names will be listed, with the 10th name being the player playing defense only. This 10th player may only bat if he moves to the DP position in the batting order.
   EXCEPTION: See Rule 4, Section 3C.

2. (Slow Pitch Only) The extra player (EP) is optional, but if one is used, it must be made known prior to the start of the game and be listed on the score sheet in the regular batting order. There will be 11 names for men's and women's slow pitch and 12 names for coed slow

pitch on the official batting order and all will bat.

3. (ADA Slow Pitch) If the physically challenged player is playing defense only (DEFO), he will be listed last on the score sheet.

B. Each player's batting and fielding record must be tabulated.

1. The first column will show the number of times at bat by each player, but a time at bat will not be charged against the player when:

(a) The player hits a sacrifice fly that scores a runner.

(b) The player is awarded a base on balls.

(c) (Fast Pitch Only) The player hits a sacrifice bunt.

(d) (Fast Pitch Only) The player is hit by a pitched ball.

(e) (Fast Pitch Only) The player hits a sacrifice slap hit.

NOTE: A slap hit is defined as a fake bunt followed by a controlled swing and resulting in the runner(s) advancing, as in the case of a sacrifice bunt.

2. The second column will show the number of runs scored by each player.

3. The third column will show the number of base hits made by each player. A base hit is a batted ball that permits the batter to reach base safely:

(a) On a fair ball which settles on the ground, clears the fence or strikes the fence before being touched by a fielder.

(b) On a fair ball which is hit with such force or such slowness or which takes such an unnatural bounce that it is impossible to field with ordinary effort in time to retire the runner.

      (c) When a fair ball which has not been touched by a fielder becomes dead because of touching the person or clothing of a runner or umpire.

      (d) When a fielder unsuccessfully attempts to retire a preceding runner and in the scorer's judgment, the batter-runner would not have been retired at first base by perfect fielding.

      (e) The player is awarded first base because of interference or obstruction.

4. The fourth column will show the number of opponents put out by each player.

      (a) A putout is credited to a fielder each time he:

          (1) Catches a fly ball or line drive.

          (2) Catches a thrown ball which retires a batter-runner or runner.

          (3) Touches a runner with ball when the runner is off the base to which the runner is entitled.

          (4) Is nearest the ball when a runner is declared out for being struck by a fair batted ball or for interference with a fielder, or when a runner is called out for being in violation of Rule 8, Sections 8E, J, S, or T.

          (5) Is the nearest fielder to an unreported substitute who is declared out in accordance with Rule 4, Section 6B OFFENSE 1(b).

      (b) A putout is credited to the catcher:

          (1) When a third strike is called.

          (2) (Slow Pitch Only) When the batter bunts or chops the ball.

        (3) When the batter fails to bat in correct order.

        (4) When the batter interferes with the catcher.

        (5) (Slow Pitch Only) When the batter hits a third strike foul ball.

        (6) (Slow Pitch Only) When a batter hits a home run in excess of the limit.

5. The fifth column shall show the number of assists made by each player. An assist shall be credited:

    (a) To each player who handles the ball in any series of plays which results in the putout of a runner or batter-runner. Only one assist shall be given to any player who handles the ball on any putout. The player who makes the putout in a rundown or similar type play shall be credited with both an assist and a putout.

    (b) To each player who handles or throws the ball in such a manner that a putout would have resulted except for an error of a teammate.

    (c) To each player who, by deflecting a batted ball, aids in a putout.

    (d) To each player who handles the ball on a play which results in a runner or batter-runner being called out for interference or for running out of the baseline.

6. The sixth column will show the number of errors made by each player. Errors are recorded:

    (a) For each player who commits a misplay which prolongs the turn at bat of the batter or the life of a present runner.

    (b) For the fielder who fails to touch a base

after receiving a thrown ball to retire a runner on a force out, or when a runner is compelled to return to a base, and provided the thrown ball could be caught by the fielder with ordinary effort.

(c) For the catcher if a batter is awarded first base because of catcher obstruction.

(d) For the fielder who fails to complete a double play because of a dropped ball.

(e) For a fielder if a runner advances a base because of said fielder's failure to catch, stop or try to stop a ball accurately thrown to a base, provided there was occasion for the throw. When more than one player could receive the throw, the scorer must determine which player gets the error.

SECTION 3. A BASE HIT shall not be scored:

A. When a runner is forced out on a batted ball or would have been forced out except for a fielding error.

B. When a player fielding a batted ball retires a preceding runner with ordinary effort.

C. When a fielder fails in an attempt to retire a preceding runner and, in the scorer's judgment, the batter-runner could have been retired at first base.

SECTION 4. A RUN BATTED IN is a run scored because of:

A. A safe hit.

B. A sacrifice bunt (Fast Pitch), a sacrifice slap hit (Fast Pitch) or a sacrifice fly (Fast Pitch and Slow Pitch).

C. An infield putout or fielder's choice.

D. A runner forced home because of obstruction, a hit batter or a base on balls.

E. A home run and all runs scored as a result.

F. Subject to the provisions of Rule 11, Section 4G, when the batter ends a game with a safe hit which drives in as many runs as are necessary to put his team in the lead, the batter shall be credited with only as many bases on his hit as are advanced by the runner who scores the winning run, and then only if the batter runs out the hit for as many bases as are advanced by the runner who scores the winning run.

G. When the batter ends a game with a home run hit out of the playing field, any runners on base are entitled to score.

SECTION 5. A PITCHER SHALL BE CREDITED WITH A WIN.

A. When a starting pitcher has pitched at least four innings and the pitcher's team is not only in the lead when the pitcher is replaced but remains in the lead for the remainder of the game.

B. When a starting pitcher has pitched at least three innings and the pitcher's team scores more runs than the opposing team in a game that is terminated after five innings of play, or in a game that is terminated after his team has scored more runs in four or more innings than the opposing team has scored in five or more innings and provided that the pitcher's team is not only in the lead if the pitcher is replaced after three innings of pitching but remains in the lead for the remainder of the game.

SECTION 6. Regardless of the number of innings the pitcher has pitched, a pitcher shall be charged with a loss if he is replaced when the pitcher's team is behind in the score and fails to tie the score or gain the lead thereafter.

SECTION 7. THE SUMMARY shall list the following items in this order:

A. The score by innings and the final score.

B. The runs batted in and by whom.

C. Two-base hits and by whom.

D. Three-base hits and by whom.

E. Home runs and by whom.

F. Sacrifice flies and by whom.

G. Double plays and players participating in them.

H. Triple plays and players participating in them.

I. Number of bases on balls charged to each pitcher.

J. Number of strike outs by each pitcher.

K. Number of hits and runs allowed by each pitcher.

L. The name of the winning pitcher.

M. The name of the losing pitcher.

N. The time of the game.

O. The names of the umpires and scorers.

P. (Fast Pitch Only) Stolen bases and by whom.
NOTE: This includes a batter advancing to second base on an awarded base on balls.

Q. (Fast Pitch Only) Sacrifice bunts and by whom.

R. (Fast Pitch Only) The names of batters hit by a pitched ball and the names of the pitchers who hit them.

S. (Fast Pitch Only) The number of wild pitches charged to each pitcher.

T. (Fast Pitch Only) The number of passed balls charged to each catcher.

SECTION 8. (Fast Pitch Only) A stolen base is credited to a runner whenever he advances one base unaided by a hit, putout, force out, fielder's choice, passed ball, wild pitch, an error, illegal pitch or obstruction.

SECTION 9. All records of a forfeited game will be included in the official records except that of a pitcher's won-lost record.

SECTION 10. TIE BREAKER RULE.
In scoring, the run scored by the player starting as a runner at second base shall be charged to the defensive team and not the pitcher. Depending on the judgment of the official scorekeeper, a run scored by any other player will be charged to the pitcher's ERA.

SECTION 12 - USE OF ASA PLAYING RULES

The ASA Softball Playing Rules shall only apply to ASA Championship Play. Provided, however, in accordance with Article 204(B) of the ASA Code, ASA State/Metro Associations as well as other organizations may adopt or use all or any part of the SAS Softball Playing Rules as they deem appropriate for use in non-Championship Play. The use of all or any part of such rules is strictly a local matter and such rules may be altered as league officials deem appropriate or necessary to conduct non-Championship Play.

Softball
Official Rules

Part Two
POINTS
OF EMPHASIS

1. **APPEALS.**
   A. **Types.**
      1. Missing a base or touching the white portion only of the double base when a play is being made on the batter-runner at first base. EXCEPTION: A play from foul territory.
      2. Leaving a base on a caught fly ball before the ball is first touched.
      3. Batting out of order.
      4. Attempting to advance to second base after making the turn at first base.
      5. (Seniors) Ineligible Courtesy Runner.
   B. **Live.** In all games an appeal may be made during a live ball by any fielder in possession of the ball touching the base missed or left too soon on a caught fly ball, or by tagging the runner committing the violation if he is still on the playing field.
   C. **Dead.** The dead ball appeal may be made: 1) Once all runners have completed their advancement and time has been called. Any infielder (including the pitcher or catcher), with or without the ball, may make a verbal appeal on a runner missing a base or leaving a base too soon on a caught fly ball. The administering umpire should then make a decision on the play. 2) If the ball has gone out of play, runners must be given the opportunity to complete their base running responsibilities, before the dead ball appeal can be made.
   D. **May Not Return.** A runner may not return to touch a missed base or one left too soon on a caught fly ball if:
      1. He has left the field of play, or
      2. A following runner has scored.
   E. **When.** Appeals must be made (1) before the next legal or illegal pitch, (2) at the end of an inning, before the pitcher and all infielders have clearly

vacated their normal fielding positions and have left fair territory on their way to the bench or dugout area, or (3) on the last play of the game, an appeal can be made until the umpires leave the field of play.

F. **Advance.** Runners may advance during a live ball appeal play. If the ball is not dead in fast pitch, each runner may leave his base when (1) the pitcher no longer has possession of the ball within eight feet of the pitcher's plate, or (2) when the pitcher makes a play on any runner (a fake throwing motion is considered a play). If time out is requested for an appeal, the umpire should grant it in either fast pitch or slow pitch, and runners may not advance until the next pitch.

G. **More Than One Appeal.** More than one appeal play may be made but guessing games should not be allowed.

EXAMPLE: The runner misses second base by a step but just touches the corner of third base. Even though an appeal is made at third (the umpire called the runner safe), an appeal may be made at second on the same runner.

H. **Awards.** An appeal must be honored even if the base missed was before or after an award.

I. **Plate and Missed Tag.** If a runner misses home plate and the catcher misses the tag, the umpire should hesitate slightly. If no tag is made, he should declare the runner safe. If an appeal play is then made by tagging either the runner or home plate, the umpire should then make a decision on this appeal play.

J. **Force Out.** If an appeal is honored at a base to which a runner was forced to advance and the out is a force out, no runs would score if it was the third out. If a forced runner, after touching the next base, retreats for any reason towards the base he had first occupied, the force play is reinstated and he may again be put out if the defense tags the base to which he is forced. NOTE: If the batter-runner is put out or is the first out on multiple outs on the same play, this would eliminate all force outs.

K. **Tag-Ups.** If a runner leaves a base too soon on a caught fly ball and returns in an attempt to retag, this is considered a time play and not a force out. If the appeal is the third out, all runs scored by runners in advance of the appealed runner and scored ahead of the legal appeal would count.

L. **Missing First Base Before the Throw Arrives.** If a runner passes first base before the throw arrives, he is considered to have touched the base unless an appeal play is made. **If using the double base and a batter-runner touches the white rather than the colored portion and a play is made at first, the same procedure follows. If an appeal is made in either situation, it must be made prior to the runner returning to first base while the ball is alive.**

M. **Fourth Out Appeal.** An appeal may be made after the third out as long as it is made properly. (i.e., One out with runner on first and third. The batter hits a fly ball that is caught. Each runner leaves his base before the caught ball is touched. An appeal is made at first base for the third out. The defensive team then makes an appeal at third base before the infielders leave the infield. The runner on third would then be declared out also, and the run would not count.

N. **End of Game.** If any situation arises which could lead to an appeal by the defense on the last play of the game, umpires should wait until all defensive infielders have crossed the foul line on their way to the team dugout, before leaving the infield. If the teams line up for high fives there is little chance for an appeal even if the defensive infielders have not crossed the foul line and umpires can leave the game at this point. No appeal can be made once the umpires have left the field.

2. BALL ROTATION PROCEDURE.

A ball rotation procedure is used in championship play and many local associations are now following the same procedure. Listed below is this procedure.

The pitcher has a choice of which ball to use at the start of each inning. If both balls do not get into play in the first half of the first inning, the pitcher in the bottom half of the first inning MUST throw the unused ball. No choice is offered.

The current game ball must be used until such time as it goes out of play or becomes unplayable. When the ball goes out of play, the umpire will throw a new ball to the pitcher. If the pitcher does not like that ball, remove it from the game and give him another ball. An umpire should never take a ball back from the pitcher and put it in his ball bag unless it is at the start of the inning when the pitcher is selecting his game ball.

After an inning is completed, the ball should be returned to the vicinity of the pitching plate by the team leaving the field or the umpire. The pitcher taking the field now has a ball with which to start the next half inning. The pitcher may request the other ball from the plate umpire, but should throw the first ball to the umpire prior to receiving the second ball. He should not have both game balls in his possession when making his choice.

3. BAT WITH DENTS.

In determining whether a bat with a dent should be legal or not, an umpire should utilize his/her bat ring to slide over the barrel of the bat. Should the bat ring continue to slide over the entire barrel, the bat would be legal. If the bat ring will not slide over the barrel, the bat would not be legal, and cannot be used. The intent of this rule is that bats should not have a flat surface where the ball could be hit. If the bat ring is able to slide over the barrel, the dent has not flattened the barrel and would not violate the intent of the rule.

4. **BATTING WITH AN ILLEGAL BAT.**
   If a batter uses an illegal (or altered) bat and reeives a base hit, and the next batter plans to use the same bat, the following penalty is now enforced. If noticed before a pitch is thrown to the second batter, the umpire will rule the batter who used the bat and is now on base out (if an altered bat, this player is now ejected from the game), the bat is removed from the game, and return all runners who advanced as a result of the hit. There is no penalty for the current batter unless a pitch is thrown to this batter, then he is the one called out (and ejected), and the first player using the illegal bat has no penalty.

5. **BATTER REMAINS IN BATTER'S BOX (JUNIOR OLYMPIC RULE ONLY).**
   This rule is not intended to penalize the youth player, but to be used to speed up the game. The batter can still obtain a signal with one foot in the box and take a practice swing, however, the batter cannot step out of the box with both feet for these purposes. The batter may leave the box should there be a play made on the bases or on the batter-runner, time out is called, if the ball is hit fair or foul, on a wild pitch or passed ball, on a swing, a slap or a check swing, or on a three ball pitch that the batter thinks is a ball, but the umpire rules a strike. If the batter leaves the box illegally, a warning should be given. Any

number of warnings on the same batter can be given. A strike should not be called without a warning. One, two or three strikes can be called on the same batter under this ruling.

6. **BATTING OUT OF THE BATTER'S BOX.**
   In order for the batter to be called out for batting out of the batter's box, one foot or both feet must be on the ground completely outside the lines of the box when contact is made with the ball. The lines of the batter's box are considered inside the box. The batter is to be called out if any part of a foot is touching home plate when he contacts the ball even though he may be touching the lines of the batter's box.

   Hitting the ball while out of the batter's box should be called immediately. The ball is dead. The batter is out whether the ball is fair or foul. In cases where there are no batter's box lines evident, good judgment must be used and the benefit of any doubt must go to the batter.

7. **CATCHER'S BOX.**
   The catcher's box is described in Rule 2, Section 3 D.

   (Slow Pitch Only) The catcher may not have any part of his body or equipment touching the ground outside the lines of the catcher's box until the ball is batted, touches the ground or plate, or reaches the catcher's box. It is a violation of Rule 6, Section 6 A and an illegal pitch if the catcher touches the ground outside the lines of the catcher's box, including home plate. The intent of this rule is to prevent catcher's obstruction. Even if the catcher is legally within the catcher's box, he may not obstruct the batter.

   (Fast Pitch Only) Catchers must remain in the catcher's

box until the pitch is released. During a regular pitch to a
batter, should the batter be in the front of the batter's
box, the catcher can move closer to the plate without
penalty. At all times, the catcher must still avoid catcher's
obstruction as the batter legally has the right to the entire
batter's box.

Obstruction does not require contact between the
catcher and the bat or batter. The umpire's request for
the catcher to move farther away from the batter to avoid
injury or obstruction should always be obeyed. (See
catcher obstruction under POE #24.)

8. CHECK SWING/BUNT STRIKE.
Normally, there are four areas which constitute whether
or not the batter has swung at the ball or checked the
swing. (1) Did he roll his wrists? (2) Did he swing
through the ball and bring the bat back, unless the batter
draws the bat back before the pitch arrives? (3) Was the
bat out in front of the body? (4) Did he make an attempt
to hit the pitch?

On a bunt attempt where the batter puts the bat across
the plate, unless the batter moves the bat towards the
ball, a strike would not be called if the ball is out of the
strike zone.

In each situation, the umpire thinks in terms of priori-
ties. First, was the pitch in the strike zone? If so, it is simply a strike. Second, did the batter swing at the pitched
ball or in the case of a bunt attempt, did he move the bat
toward the pitched ball? In either case, it is the plate
umpire's call. If in doubt or if blocked out, he will call
the pitch a ball. Umpires will not call the pitch a strike
unless it was in the strike zone or the batter swung at the
ball. If the umpire calls the pitch a ball and the catcher

requests help, the umpire should ask for help. On a missed bunt attempt with two strikes, the dropped third strike rule will apply. (Rule 8, Section 1 B)

9. **COMMUNICATION DEVICES.**

No form of communication devices are allowed on the playing field or in the dugouts. Teams have used head or ear phones between coaches at first and third base, between coaches and the dugout, and from the stands to the dugout. Some teams have been found to steal signals (catcher to pitcher in fast pitch, etc.) while outside the field of play (stands or outfield area) and communicated with coaches or players. Umpires should prohibit usage of any such equipment.

10. **CONFERENCES.**

A. **Defensive.** A defensive charged conference takes place when the defense requests a suspension of play for any reason, and a representative enters the playing field and confers with the pitcher. The intent of this rule is to reduce delays in the game. It is also a conference if the team representative confers with another player who, prior to a pitch being thrown, confers with the pitcher. The umpire should advise the team representative when he declares a charged conference. The penalty for a second charged conference with the same pitcher in one inning is removal of the pitcher from the pitching position for the duration of the game. If the pitcher returns to the pitching position after being removed and one pitch has been thrown, the pitcher is ejected from the game.

The following are not defensive conferences:

  1. If the team representative informs an umpire prior to crossing the foul line that he is removing the pitcher, and he does so.

2. Shouting instructions from the dugout area to the pitcher.

3. If a dugout representative confers with a pitcher during a charged offensive conference and is ready to play ball when the offense is ready.

4. A manager playing in the game may confer with the pitcher and is not charged; however, an umpire may control repeated meetings between a playing manager and a pitcher by first issuing a warning and then ejecting the manager.

B. **Offensive.** An offensive charged conference occurs when an offensive team requests a suspension of play and is granted time by an umpire to permit a team representative (usually the manager or coach) to confer with a batter and/or runner(s). Only one such conference is allowed per inning. The umpires should refuse to grant the second conference.

PENALTY: If the offensive team insists on holding a second conference in an inning after being informed by the umpire that it is not permitted, the umpire should eject the team representative from the game. The following are not offensive conferences:

1. A team representative confers with a batter and/or runner(s) during a defensive charged conference and is ready to play when the defense is.

2. If the pitcher is putting on a warm-up jacket.

C. **Super Slow Pitch. A defensive conference is charged any time a manager or representative from the dugout goes onto the field to speak with any player. A team is allowed only three for the entire game. Each conference after the third shall result in the pitcher being removed from the pitching position for the remainder of the game.**

D. **Officials.** It will not be a charged conference to either team when time-out is called by the umpire for an official reason. (e.g. An injured player, blood rule, scorekeeper problems, field maintenance repairs, etc.) A coach may confer with a pitcher, batter, or a runner during the official's time-out without penalty as long as they are ready to continue once the problem has been resolved.

11. DELAYED DEAD BALL.

There are five situations when a violation of a rule occurs, it is recognized by an umpire and the ball remains live until the conclusion of the play. These situations are:

A. An illegal pitch. (Rule 6, Section 1-8 • Fast Pitch and Modified Pitch) (Rule 6, Section 1-7 • Slow Pitch and 16-Inch Slow Pitch)
B. Catcher's obstruction. (Rule 8, Section 1 D)
C. Plate umpire interference. (Rule 8, Section 7 F)
D. Obstruction. (Rule 8, Section 6 B)
E. Batted or thrown ball contacted by detached equipment. (Rule 8, Section 6 F)

NOTE: Once the entire play is completed in each situation, the proper enforcement should be made.

12. CRASHING INTO A FIELDER WITH THE BALL.
(Interference)

In order to prevent injury and protect the defensive player attempting to make a play on a runner, the runner must be called out if he remains on his feet and crashes into a defensive player holding the ball and waiting to apply a tag, or if the defensive player is about to receive a thrown ball. In order to prevent the crash ruling, the runner can slide, jump over the top of the defender holding the ball, go around the defender (if outside the three-foot lane, the runner would be called out), or return to the previous base touched.

NOTE: If the act is determined to be flagrant, the offender will be ejected. A runner may slide into the fielder.

A. When a runner is called out for crashing into a fielder holding the ball, the ball becomes dead. Each runner must return to the last base touched at the time of interference.

B. If, in A above, the runner crashed into a fielder holding the ball before he was put out and, in the judgment of the umpire, it was an attempt to break up an obvious double play, the immediate succeeding runner will also be declared out under Rule 8, Section 8 J.

C. If the crash occurs after the runner was called out, the runner closest to home plate will be declared out under Rule 8, Section 8 P.

D. If an obstructed runner crashes into a fielder holding the ball, the obstruction call will be ignored and the runner will be called out under Rule 8, Section 8 Q. An award of this type under Rule 8, Section 6 B (1 and 2) does not give the runner the right to violate Rule 8, Section 8 Q.

E. If a defensive player is fielding a thrown ball and the flight of the ball carries or draws him into the path of the base runner, this would not be a crash.

F. If the ball, runner and the defensive player all arrive at the same time and contact is made, the umpire should not invoke the collision rule (interference) or obstruction. This is merely incidental contact. If the ball does not enter dead ball territory in either E or F, the ball remains live and in play.

13. **DESIGNATED PLAYER OR DP (Fast Pitch Only).** This individual can be listed in any of the nine spots in the batting order. The player listed number 10 in the lineup (who plays defense only) will be called the DEFO.

A. A designated player (DP) may be used for any player provided it is made known prior to the start of the game and the player's name is indicated on the line-up as one of the nine hitters in the batting order.

B. The name of the player for whom the DP is batting (DEFO) will be placed in the 10th position in the line-up.

C. The DP and any substitutes for the DP must remain in the same position in the batting order for the entire game. The DEFO and any substitutes for the DEFO must enter or leave the game in the 10th position in the line-up.

D. The DP may be substituted for at any time either by a pinch hitter or pinch runner. This player becomes the DP and has all the options of the DP position. The starting DP and a substitute for the DP can never be in the game at the same time.

E. The DEFO may be substituted for at any time. This player becomes the DEFO and has all the options of the DEFO position. The starting DEFO and a substitute for the DEFO can never be in the game at the same time.

F. The DP may be replaced by the DEFO as a hitter or as a runner. This reduces the number of players in the game from ten to nine and must be reported to the umpire since the DP has left the game. The DP and the DEFO can never be on offense at the same time.

G. The DEFO may be replaced on defense by the DP. This reduces the number of players in the game from ten to nine and must be reported to the umpire since the DEFO has left the game. The DP and the DEFO can be on defense at the same time.

H. The starting DP may re-enter the game one time and must return to the original DP position in the batting order. If the DP re-enters and the DEFO was batting in the DP position, the DEFO shall return to the number 10 position in the line-up, play defense only and is not considered to have left the game.

I. The starting DEFO may re-enter the game one time and must return to the original DEFO position (number 10 in the line-up). If the DEFO re-enters and the DP was playing defense in the DEFO position, the DP shall continue to bat in the DP position of the batting order, play offense only or play defense for another player and is not considered to have left the game.

J. The DP may play defense for any player at any position. a) Should the DP play defense for a player other than the one for whom the DP is batting (DEFO), that player (the position player) will continue to bat, but not play defense and is not considered to have left the game.

K. The role of the DP/DEFO is never terminated. A team may go from ten to nine players and back to ten players any number of times during the game. The game may end with nine or ten players. Violations of the DP Rule happen when:

    1. Placing the DP on defense for the DEFO must be reported to the umpire. PENALTY FOR NOT REPORTING:

        a) Eject the DP.

        b) Secure a replacement for the DP position. This can be (1) a legal substitute, (2) the starting DP re-entering (if he was not the one ejected), or (3) the DEFO batting in the DP position.

        c) Secure a replacement for the DEFO position (number 10 in the line-up). This can

be (1) a legal substitute, (2) the starting
DEFO re-entering, or (3) the DP replacement playing defense for the DEFO.

2. Placing the DEFO on offense for the DP must
be reported to the umpire. PENALTY FOR
NOT REPORTING:
   a) Eject the DEFO.
   b) Secure a replacement for the DEFO position (number 10 in the line-up). This can
   be (1) a legal substitute, (2) the starting
   DEFO re-entering (if he was not the one
   ejected), or (3) the DP playing defense
   for the DEFO.
   c) Secure a replacement for the DP position
   (number 10 in the line-up). This can be
   (1) a legal substitute, (2) the starting DP
   re-entering, or (3) the DEFO replacement batting in the DP position.

3. Placing the DEFO into one of the first nine batting positions other than the DP position is illegal. PENALTY:
   a) Eject the DEFO.
   b) Secure a replacement for the DEFO position (number 10 in the line-up). This can
   be (1) a legal substitute, (2) the starting
   DEFO re-entering (if he was not the one
   ejected), or (3) the DP playing defense
   for the DEFO.
   c) Secure a replacement for the batting position where the DEFO erroneously batted.
   This can be (1) a legal substitute or (2)
   the starting player re-entering.

NOTE: For a regular substitution and re-entry, and
for determining when a batter is called out, when run-

ners return, and when managers are given an option, the penalties for unreported or illegal substitutions are in effect.

14. DUGOUT CONDUCT.

This rule reflects on coaches, players, substitutes, or other bench personnel. Once the game begins, all players other than those involved in the game (all defensive players, and on offense only the on-deck batter and base coaches) cannot be outside the dugout except when the rule allows or the reason is justified by the umpire. Managers walking on the field for a conference is an example of a rule allowing a coach or player on the field, or if one of those in the dugout has to go to the restroom, this is an example of umpire justification. Players cannot be out of the dugout between innings standing near the batter's box observing the pitcher warming up (unless it is the on-deck batter), nor can they step outside the dugout to have a smoke or to observe the game from behind backstop or side screen.

15. EQUIPMENT ON THE PLAYING FIELD.

No loose equipment, miscellaneous items or a detached part of a player's uniform, other than that being legally used in the game at the time, should be within playable territory. Official equipment which may be within playable territory with no penalty includes the batter's bat, the catcher's mask, umpire paraphernalia, any helmet which has inadvertently fallen off on an offensive or defensive player during the course of play or any equipment belonging to a person assigned to the game. Loose gloves, hats, helmets, jackets, balls (including the on-deck batter's bat), or any other loose equipment, miscellaneous item or detached uniform part which are within playable territory and are not being legally used in the game at the time could cause a blocked ball or interference.

A. **Thrown Ball.**
   1. If a thrown ball hits loose equipment belonging to the team at bat, a dead ball is declared immediately. If such action interferes with a play, interference is ruled. The ball is dead, the runner being played on at the time of the interference shall be declared out, and each runner must return to the last base touched prior to the thrown ball hitting the loose equipment. If no apparent play is obvious, a blocked ball is ruled, no one is called out, and all runners must return to the last base touched at the time of the dead ball declaration.
   2. If the loose equipment belongs to the team in the field, it becomes a blocked ball and the overthrow rule applies.

B. **Batted Ball.**
   1. A batted foul ball touching loose equipment is a foul ball.
   2. A batted fair ball touching loose equipment belonging to (a) the offense is considered a dead ball and runners return, unless they are forced to advance when the batter-runner is awarded first base on the base hit or (b) the defense is considered a dead ball and all runners, including the batter-runner, are awarded two bases from their position at the time of the pitch.

C. **Batted Fly Ball Hitting Bird.**
   If the ball drops and is caught by a defensive player, the ball remains live and a legal catch should be ruled.

16. **EXTRA PLAYER OR EP (Slow Pitch Only).**
   If a team uses the EP, it must be on the lineup card at the start of the game, and the team must end the game with

11 players or forfeit.
EXCEPTION: short-handed team ruling.

All 11 players bat but only 10 play defense. Changes with the defensive players may be made at any time; however, the batting order may not change. (e.g., The EP may sit on the bench one inning, play third base one inning, play outfield one inning, sit on the bench again and then play first base. All would be legal as long as the EP remained in his same position in the batting order. This would be the same for any of the starting 11 players.).

Any of the starting 11 players may leave the game once and re-enter. A starting player and his substitute may not be in the game at the same time. If this occurs, the player listed in the wrong spot in the batting order is ejected by the umpire.

17. **FAKE TAG.**
   A. A fake tag occurs when a fielder without the ball deceives the runner by impeding his progress (i.e., causing him to slide, slow down or stop running).
      1. Obstruction is called when a fake tag is made as mentioned above. The umpire shall give the delayed dead ball signal and let the play continue to its completion. The obstructed runner, and each runner affected by the obstruction, will always be awarded the base or bases he would have reached if there had not been any obstruction under Rule 8, Section 6 B 3. Remember, each runner is awarded a base or bases only, if in the judgment of the umpire, he would have made the base or bases had there not been any obstruction.
      2. The umpire should rule obstruction on a fake tag. Continued fake tags should result in ejec-

tions. In flagrant cases where the sliding player gets hurt, the offending player should be ejected without warning.

3. If a fielder fakes a tag but the runner continues on to the next base without sliding or breaking stride, there is not a rule violation. Obstruction is the act of a fielder in the base path without the ball impeding the progress of a runner. In this case, the progress was not impeded. A warning should be given.

18. FALLING OVER THE FENCE ON A CATCH.

The fence is an extension of the playing field, making it legal for a player to climb and make the catch. If he catches a ball in the air and his momentum carries him through or over the fence, the catch is good, the batter-runner is out, the ball is dead, and with fewer than two outs, all runners are advanced one base without liability to be put out. Guidelines are (1) if he catches the ball before he touches the ground outside the playing area, the catch is legal, or (2) if he catches the ball after he touches the ground outside the playing area, it is not a catch. If a portable fence is used which is collapsible and a defensive player is standing on the fence, it is ruled a good catch. A defensive player can climb a fence to make a catch, so he should be able to stand on a fence which has fallen to the ground. There should be no doubt left in an umpire's judgment whether the fence is on the ground, or three feet off the ground when the defender steps on it. As long as the defensive player has not stepped outside the playing area (other side of the fence), the catch will be good.

19. HITTING THE BALL A SECOND TIME.

When an umpire considers the act of a batter hitting the

ball a second time, he should place the act into one of three categories.

A. If the bat is in the hands of the batter when the ball comes in contact with it, and the batter is in the batter's box, it is a foul ball. If an entire foot of the batter is completely outside the batter's box, he is out. When in doubt, don't guess the batter out. Call it a foul ball.

B. If the bat is out of the batter's hands (dropped or thrown) and it hits the ball in fair territory, the ball is dead and the batter-runner is out. If the ball hits the bat on the ground, the batter is not out. The umpire should then determine whether the ball is fair or foul based on the fair/foul rule. If the ball rolls against the bat in fair territory, it remains live. If it stops or is touched in fair territory, it is a fair ball. If it touches the bat in fair territory and then rolls to foul ground and stops, it is a foul ball. If the ball rolls against the bat in foul territory, it is a foul ball regardless.

C. If a batter swings and misses the pitched ball but (a) accidentally hits it on the follow-through, (b) intentionally hits it on the second swing, or (c) hits the ball after it bounces off the catcher or his mitt, the ball is dead, and all runners must return to the base they occupied prior to th epitch. (FP and 16" SP only) in (b) and (c) if the act is intentional with runners on base, the batter will be called out for intereference. If this occurs on strike three in fast pitch, Rule 8 Section 2 F has precedence.

20. **HOME RUNS (SLOW PITCH) AND RUNNING BASES.**
   This rule applies only to games involving Men's Major, Men's Major Industrial, Men's Major Church, and Super Slow Pitch Divisions. When a home run is hit out of the ball park, the batter and all base runners can

go directly to the dugout. No appeals can be made for runners missing a base. This speeds the game as batters do not have to run the 260 feet (or 280 feet in Super SP) and players/coaches do not gather around home plate to congratulate the home run hitter.

21. IMAGINARY LINE OR DEAD BALL AREA.

When a fielder carries a live ball into a dead ball area, the ball becomes dead and a base or bases are awarded to all baserunners. If the act is unintentional, the award is one base. If the act is intentional, the award is two bases. The base award is governed from the last base legally touched at the time the ball became dead.

If a chalk line is used to determine an out-of-play area, the line is considered in play. If a fielder is touching the line, he is considered in the field of play and may make a legal catch or throw. If either foot is on the ground completely in dead ball territory (not touching the line), the ball becomes dead and no play may be made.

If a player has one foot inside the line or touching the line, and another foot in the air at the time the catch is made, the catch is good and the batter is out. If the fielder then steps into a dead ball area (foot on the ground), the ball becomes dead and all baserunners are awarded one base from the last base touched when the ball became dead.

22. INTENTIONALLY DROPPED BALL.

The ball cannot be intentionally dropped unless the fielder has actually caught and then dropped it. Merely guiding the ball to the ground should not be considered an intentionally dropped ball.

23. INTENTIONAL WALK (Fast Pitch Only).

The ball is live during an intentional walk in fast pitch.

All defensive players must be in fair territory until the pitch is released, except the catcher, who must remain in the catcher's box, and the pitcher, who must be in a legal pitching position at the start of each pitch. If they do not position themselves in fair territory, an illegal pitch should be called for each pitch thrown while any member of the defense is standing in foul territory. In fast pitch, the pitches must be thrown to the catcher.

24. INTENTIONAL WALK (Slow Pitch Only).

Because the ball is dead when it crosses the plate and no play may be made, it is permissible for the batter to be walked intentionally if the umpire is notified by the pitcher. If two successive batters are to be walked, the plate umpire will not award the second intentional walk until the first batter reaches first base. (Rule 8, Section 1 C 2)

25. INTERFERENCE.

Interference is defined as the act of an offensive player or team member which impedes, hinders or confuses a defensive player attempting to execute a play. It may be in the form of physical contact, verbal distraction, visual distraction, or any type of distraction which would hinder the fielder in the execution of the play. Defensive players must be given the opportunity to field the ball anywhere on the playing field or throw the ball without being hindered.

A. Runner interference includes: a runner or batter-runner who interferes with 1) a fielder executing a play, 2) a runner or batter-runner who is hit by a fair untouched batted ball or 3) intentionally interfering with a thrown ball.

    1. When a runner interferes with a fielder, the umpire must determine if the interference occurred before or after the runner who interfered was put out and then apply the proper rule.

2. When a runner is hit by a fair batted ball, it is interference if it occurred before it passed an infielder (excluding the pitcher) or after it passed an infielder (if **another fielder** had a chance to make an out), and provided the runner was not in contact with the base. It is not interference if the batted ball touched or was touched by a player before it hit the runner, or if the runner was standing in foul territory.

3. A runner could be standing on a base and a defensive player bumps the runner while watching the flight of the ball. If the defensive player fails to make a catch on a catchable ball, it is the umpire's judgment whether interference should or should not be called. The rule provides that a runner must vacate any space needed by a fielder to make a play on a batted ball, unless the runner has contact with a legally occupied base when the hindrance occurs. In this case, the runner should not be called out unless the hindrance is intentional.

4. If interference occurs by the runner on a foul fly ball not caught, the runner is out, a strike is called, the ball is dead, and the batter remains at bat. (Slow Pitch Only) If on the third strike, it would be two outs.

5. For crash interference, refer to POE #10.

B. Batter interference occurs while the batter is at bat and before he hits the ball. It occurs in fast pitch when the batter intentionally interferes with the catcher's throw on an attempted steal or when he interferes with the catcher on a play at the plate. The batter's box is not a sanctuary for the batter when a play is being made at the plate. It could also occur when a batter releases his bat in such a manner that it

hits the catcher and prevents him from making a play.
If the batter merely drops his bat and the catcher trips
over it, there is no interference. Batter interference is
also described in POE #16B.

C. On-deck batters may be charged with interference if
they interfere with a throw and a possible tag on a
runner, or a fielder's opportunity to make an out on a
fly ball.

D. Coach's interference occurs when a base coach runs
toward home and draws a throw, or when he interferes with a fielder attempting to catch or throw a
ball. The coach's box is not a sanctuary.

E. Spectator interference occurs when a spectator:

    1) Enters the field and interferes with a play
       EFFECT: the batter and runner(s) shall be
       placed where in the umpire's judgment they
       would have made, had the interference not
       occurred. The field belongs to the fielder and
       the stands belong to the spectator.

    2) Reaches onto the field from the stands and pre-
       vents a fielder from catching a fly ball in the
       field of play.
       EFFECT: A dead ball is ruled and the batter is
       called out. All runners are returned to the base
       at the start of the pitch. It is not interference if
       the fielder reaches into the stands.

F. Umpire interference occurs (1) (Fast Pitch & Slow
Pitch) when an umpire is hit by a fair, untouched batted ball before it passes an infielder (excluding the
pitcher). The batter-runner is awarded first base (exception to the statement that someone must be called out
on interference). (2) (Fast Pitch Only) when an umpire
interferes with a catcher's attempt to put out a runner
stealing, or an attempted pick-off from the catcher to

any base. It is interference only if the runner is not put out, in which case he is returned to his base. In no other case is umpire interference ruled.

When batter, batter-runner, runner, on-deck batter or coach interference occurs, the ball is dead, someone must be called out, and each other runner must return to the last base touched at the time of the interference.

G. Offensive team interference could occur on a thrown ball striking loose equipment left on the playing field should there actually be a play interfered with (See POE #12.)

26. LOOK-BACK RULE (Fast Pitch Only) (Rule 8 Section 8 T).

When a runner is legitimately off his base after a pitch, or as a result of a batter completing his turn at bat, and is stationary when the pitcher has the ball in the circle, the runner must immediately attempt to advance to the next base or immediately return to the base left.

The responsibility is completely on the runner. There is no obligation on the pitcher to look, fake or throw.

A. Failure to immediately proceed nonstop to the next base or return to his original base after the pitcher has the ball within the circle will result in the runner being declared out.

B. Once the runner has returned to or stops at any base for any reason, he will be declared out if he leaves said base

EXCEPTION A-B: A runner will not be declared out if: (1) a play is made on him or another runner, (2) the pitcher leaves the circle or drops the ball, or (3) the pitcher releases the ball to the batter.

C. If two runners are off base and two different umpires call each runner out, they must determine which runner was called out first and return the other runner to the base he left.

D. When a runner has been declared out, the ball is ruled dead. It is not possible to obtain two outs on the "look back" rule.

E. **A pitcher fielding a ball in the circle is just another fielder and runners can leave their base. If they leave their base, the same rule applies while the pitcher holds the ball in the circle: once the runner stops, they must decide which way to continue or be called out.**

A base on balls or a dropped third strike is treated as a batted ball as long as the batter-runner continues past first base. For scoring purposes, when he advances to second base, it is considered a stolen base. If he stops at first base, however, and then steps off the base after the pitcher has the ball within the circle, he is out. Should the batter-runner overrun first base, turn towards first after rounding the base, does not stop, but he advances towards second base, this is legal as long as the runner has not retouched first base on the way to second base. If he does retouch first base on the way to second base, he should be called out.

If the runner is moving toward any base when the pitcher receives the ball in the circle, that runner may continue toward that base and is allowed to stop once, then must immediately attempt to advance to the next base or immediately return to the base left. If, after the pitcher has the ball within the circle, the runner starts back to his original base or forward to another base and then stops or reverses direction, he is out, unless the pitcher makes a play on him. When a play is made on a runner, he may stop or reverse his direction.

The runner is out if he stands off his base and does not immediately attempt to advance or return after the pitcher has the ball within the circle.

Any act by the pitcher in possession of the ball in the circle that, in the umpire's judgment, causes the runner to react; is considered making a play.

NOTE: Being in the eight-foot circle is defined as both feet within or partially within the lines. The pitcher is not considered in the circle if either foot is completely outside the lines.

27. MEDIA COVERAGE.

Media authorized by the tournament committee can be on the playing field but must not use tripods. All media personnel must be able to move to avoid being hit by an overthrown or batted ball. Should they accidentally be hit, the ball remains live. All photographic equipment must be on the photographer. No equipment can be left on the ground.

28. OBSTRUCTION.

Obstruction is the act of a fielder (1) not in possession of the ball, (2) not in the act of fielding a batted ball, or (3) not about to receive a thrown ball which impedes the progress of a batter-runner or runner who is legally running the bases.

NOTE: In defining "not about to receive a thrown ball," the ball must be between the advancing runner and the defensive player about to make the catch and play. If the ball is outside this area and a collision occurs, obstruction is ruled. If the ball is within this area and a collision occurs, it is neither obstruction nor interference and the ball remains live.

Whenever obstruction occurs, whether a play is being made on a runner or not, the umpire will declare obstruction and signal a delayed dead ball. The ball will remain live. If the obstructed runner is put out prior to reaching the base he would have reached had there not been obstruction, a dead ball is called and the obstructed runner, and each other runner affected by the obstruction, will be awarded the base(s) he would have reached, in the umpire's judgment, had there not been obstruction. An obstructed runner could be called out between the two bases he was obstructed if he was properly appealed for missing the base or leaving a base before a fly ball was first touched. If the runner committed an act of interference after the obstruction, this too would overrule the obstruction.

When an obstructed runner is awarded a base he would have made had there been no obstruction and a preceding runner is on that base, time will be called. The obstructed runner will be awarded that base and the runner occupying it will be entitled to the next base without liability to be put out.

It should also be clear that when saying "a runner cannot be called out between the two bases he was obstructed" does not pertain when another violation is being played upon. (e.g., A runner leaving second base too soon on a fly ball is returning after the ball is caught and is obstructed between second base and third base. If the runner would not have made it back to second base prior to the throw arriving, he would remain out.)

If the obstructed runner is put out after passing the base he would have reached had there not been obstruction, he is running at his own risk and, if tagged, would be called out. The ball remains live and other plays may be made.

When the runner is obstructed during a rundown, a delayed dead ball is called. If the runner is tagged out after being obstructed, a dead ball is ruled, and he is awarded the base he would have made had there been no obstruction. If the ball is overthrown after the obstruction, the runner may advance. He may not be called out between the two bases where he was obstructed.

If other runners are advancing when an umpire calls time following a play on an obstructed runner, a rule of thumb for placement of the other runners is: If they have not reached half way to the next base, they must return to the previous base. However, if they have advanced over half way, they are allowed to advance to the next base.

Catcher obstruction is a delayed dead ball call. Should catcher obstruction be called when the batter hits the ball, and if he reaches first base safely, and if all other runners have advanced at least one base, the obstruction is cancelled. All action as a result of the batted ball stands. If he does not reach first base or if one of the other runners does not advance at least one base, the manager of the offensive team has the option of taking the result of the play or awarding the batter first base and advancing other runners only if they are forced because of the award. If catcher obstruction occurs when a batter steps out of the box on a legitimate attempt to hit the ball, the obstruction will take precedence and the penalty for catcher obstruction will be enforced. The batter must be given the opportunity to hit the ball. Should the batter delay his swing, and clearly the attempt is no longer to hit the ball out but rather to interfere with the catcher's throw on a steal attempt, then batter's interference would be the ruling. (Also see POE #5 - Catcher's Box.)

(FP Only) Any runner attempting to advance (i.e., steal or squeeze) on a catcher's obstruction of the batter shall

be awarded the base they are attempting. If a runner is not attempting to advance on the catcher's obstruction, they shall not be entitled to the next base, unless forced to advance because of the batter being awarded first base.

29. OVER-RUNNING FIRST BASE.

After over-running first base, the batter-runner may legally turn to his left or his right when returning to the base. If any attempt is made to advance to second, regardless of whether he is in fair or foul territory, he is liable for an appeal out if tagged by a defensive player with the ball while off the base.

When the double base is used, batter-runners can utilize the white portion whenever the batted ball is in the outfield, or no play is being made at first base. If a play is made at first base, but the ball is overthrown, this also allows the batter-runner to use the white if trying to advance to second base. If the batter-runner overruns first base and returns to the colored portion (rather than the white), sufficient time to touch the white should be given, particularly in youth play.

30. OVERTHROWS.

Runners are always awarded two bases on overthrows which go out of play or become blocked as a result of hitting loose equipment belonging to or a team member of the defensive team that does not belong on the field. (POE #12). Regardless of who made the throw, two bases are awarded from the last base touched at the time the ball left the hand.

Direction of runners has no bearing on the award. (i.e., When an overthrow is made on a runner returning to a base, he is awarded two bases from that base.

EXCEPTION: If he was returning to first base and the throw was from the outfield and it left the outfielder's hand while the runner was between second base and third base, but the runner was between first base and second base when the ball went out of play, the runner would be awarded home.)

The award of bases is determined by the position of the front runner if two runners are between the same bases at the time of the award. Two runners between first and second will be awarded second and third; however, if two runners are between second and third, both will be awarded home. Should the umpire make an error in the award of bases, after one pitch has been thrown to the batter (legal or illegal) the umpire cannot change the award.

When a fielder loses possession of the ball on an attempted tag and the ball then enters the dead ball area or becomes blocked, all runners are awarded one base from the last base touched at the time the ball entered the dead ball area or became blocked.

(Fast Pitch Only) On pitched balls going out of play, the runners are awarded one base from the last base touched at the time of the pitch. If a batter receives a base on balls and the fourth ball gets away from the catcher and goes out of play, he will be awarded first base only.

31. **PITCHING (Fast Pitch Only).**

   There are six basic features in the pitching rule. They are:
   A. **Contact With the Pitcher's Plate.** Male adult and JO pitchers may have only one foot in contact with the pitcher's plate. The non-pivot foot may be on or behind it. Both feet must be within the 24-inch length of said plate. Female adult and female Junior Olympic pitchers must have both feet in contact with

the pitcher's plate and within the 24-inch length of said plate.

B. **Signal.** A signal must be taken by the pitcher while one or both feet are in contact with the pitcher's plate as described in (A). The ball must be held in either hand or the glove while taking the signal. The ball held in one hand may be in front of or behind the body. Taking a signal prevents a pitcher from walking onto the pitcher's plate and putting the batter at a disadvantage by throwing a quick pitch. **The signal may be taken from the catcher or from the dugout.**

C. **Preliminary to Delivery.** In the male adult and JO competition, if the pitcher takes the signal with both feet on the plate and he wants to pitch with the non-pivot foot starting behind the plate, he may step or slide this foot backwards (1) prior to bringing the two hands together, (2) when simultaneously bringing the two hands together or (3) after bringing the two hands together. Female adult and female Junior Olympic pitchers must keep both feet in contact with the pitcher's plate during the entire preliminary process. Both: After taking the signal, the ball must be taken in both hands and held for a minimum of one second and not more than 10 seconds. The pitcher may begin the pitch once the hands are brought together. During this entire period, the pivot foot must remain in contact with the pitcher's plate. No rocking movement which pulls the pivot foot off the pitcher's plate is allowed. If the pivot foot turns or slides in order to push off the pitcher's plate, this is acceptable as long as contact is maintained. It is not considered a step if the pitcher slides his foot across the plate.

D. **Start of Pitch.** The start of the pitch begins when the pitcher takes one hand off the ball.

E. **Delivery.** The delivery may not be two full revolutions. The pitcher's hand may go past the hip twice as long as there are not two complete revolutions. The wrist may not be any farther from the hip than the elbow. The delivery may not have a stop or reversal of the forward motion.

F. **Step or Release.** A step (only one) must be taken and it must be forward, toward the batter and within the 24-inch length of the pitcher's plate. Dragging or pushing off with the pivot foot from the plate is required of female adult and female **and male** Junior Olympic pitchers. Male adult pitchers are allowed to have both feet in the air during the forward step. This leap is legal only in adult male competition. Pushing off from a spot other than the pitcher's plate is considered a crow hop and is illegal **in all adult and Junior Olympic play.** The release of the ball must be simultaneous with the step. (See Rule 1 for definitions of a crow hop and leaping.)

32. PITCHER'S UNIFORM.

A pitcher should be dressed identically to other players on the team. A long-sleeved sweatshirt of any color is acceptable under the jersey. If worn, it may not extend past the wrist so a clear gap can be seen between the ball and the end of the shirt. If two players (including the pitcher) have sweatshirts on, they must be identical in color and style. No player may wear ragged, frayed or slit sleeves on an exposed undershirt.

A pitcher may wear a batting glove and/or wristband on the glove hand and wrist. The batting glove may be white. A pitcher may wear the pitcher's toe plate on his shoe.

(Fast Pitch Only) Other than a sweatshirt, nothing can be worn below the pitching arm elbow, including a band-aid on the fingers.

(Slow Pitch Only) A pitcher may wear a wristband on his pitching arm, can have tape on the pitching fingers and wear any color fielder's glove. No batting glove can be worn on the pitching hand.

33. PROTESTED GAME UPHELD AND RESCHEDULED.

When a protested game is upheld, the game is to be rescheduled from the point at which it was protested. Although the same lineups are to be used when the game is resumed, there is no penalty for substitutions legally placed into the lineups at this time. Even if a player was not at the protested game, he is legal for substitution purposes when the game is rescheduled as long as he is on the roster. If a player was ejected in the original game after the protest was filed, that player may legally play in the rescheduled game because he was legally in the game at the time of the protest, unless the ejection also drew suspension for unsportsmanlike conduct.

34. RUN SCORING ON THE THIRD OUT OF AN INNING.

A run will not score if the third out of the inning is a putout at first base (batter-runner) or at another base if a preceding runner is forced because of the batter becoming a batter-runner.

Missed bases could result in a force out. (i.e., If the runner from first base missed second base on a base hit and that was the third out of the inning when properly appealed, any run(s) scored would not count.)

An appeal play on a runner leaving a base too soon on a caught fly ball is considered a time play and not a force. If the appeal results in the third out, any runners preceding the appealed runner would score if they crossed home plate prior to the out.

35. RUNNER HIT BY A FAIR BALL.

A. **While in Contact With the Base.** The runner will never be called out unless the act is intentional. The ball remains live or dead depending on the closest defensive player. If the closest defensive player is in front of the base the runner is in contact with, the ball is live. However, if the closest defensive player is behind the base, the ball is dead. If the ball is ruled dead and the batter awarded a base hit, all runners forced to advance due to the batter being placed on first base shall be advanced one base.

B. **While Not in Contact With the Base.** The runner will be called out or ruled safe depending on the interference rule. (Rule 8, Section 8 J & K or Rule 8, Section 9 D-F)

36. SHOES.

Metal cleats are legal in adult male or adult female fast pitch and slow pitch. They are not legal in adult coed slow pitch play, seniors play, or any level of youth fast pitch or slow pitch. Polyurethane or plastic cleats shaped to look like a metal triangle toe or heel plate are illegal in youth, seniors, and coed play also. If there are nubbins or round plastic cleats in addition to the triangle plate, the shoe is legal. Cleats that screw onto a post are illegal, but cleats that screw into the shoe are legal.

37. SHORTHANDED TEAMS.

A team may continue a game with one player less than it uses to begin a game as long as the player vacancy is not created by an ejection. This rule is designed to avoid forfeits whenever possible. In all cases, a team must have a full lineup of players to begin a contest.

In slow pitch, a team must begin with 10 (or if using an EP, with 11), however, they may continue to play with nine (or 10) if a player has to leave the game for any reason other than ejection, and they do not have a substitute on the bench. In the men's senior division where 11 or 12 players can be used, they can play with 11 under the same conditions. The same applies to fast pitch, a team must begin with nine (or if using the DP, with 10), however, they may continue to play with one less.

The following guidelines should be followed in administering this rule:

A. If a team is short one player due to a player being disqualified in Class C or D divisions for excessive home runs, the game is not forfeited. If the team is already playing shorthanded and the disqualification occurs, then the game will be forfeited.

B. If a player leaving the game is a runner, the runner is declared out even if the runner reached the base safely.

C. Whenever the absent player is due to bat, an out is declared. This is the same in coed play, therefore two males or two females cannot follow each other in the batting order without an out.

D. When a team plays shorthanded because a player leaves the game, the player cannot return to the lineup. EXCEPTION: A player being treated under the blood rule can return. (Rule 4, Section 8)

E. If there is an eligible substitute at the game, or if an eligible substitute arrives before the game is over, the substitute must enter the game.

F. A team cannot bat less than nine (slow pitch) or eight (fast pitch). The game is forfeited.
NOTE: If the team has only 10 players, one is injured in the third inning, a substitute arrives in the fifth inning and is entered in the game, and another player becomes injured, this is legal as the team can continue

to play with nine. If the same team did not have a substitute when the second person was injured, reducing the number of players to eight, the game is forfeited. Playing shorthanded is not a strategic option for a coach. The purpose of this rule is to allow all players on a team to play without fear of injury or illness that previously created a forfeit.

G. If a team is playing shorthanded and is involved in a tiebreaker, and it is the shorthanded spot in the batting order who is supposed to begin play at second base, no one out should be declared. Instead, place on second base the player whose name precedes the absent player's name in the lineup.

H. **(Slow Pitch Only) If a team begins and continues the game with nine players, they are not allowed to use the "shorthanded rule" and play with eight.**

38. STEALING (Slow Pitch).

Base stealing is illegal in slow pitch; however, the runner is not out. Since the ball is dead on balls and strikes, he is returned to the base held at the time of the pitch. Because he cannot steal, he may not be picked off either. A runner may be called out for failure to keep contact with a base to which he is entitled until a legally pitched ball is batted, touches the ground or has reached home plate.

An exception to this rule is in the Super Slow Pitch **and Major Men's Slow Pitch games only.** Stealing is permitted as long as the runner does not leave his base until the ball reaches home plate. If the ball touches the ground prior to reaching home plate, the ball is dead and the runner cannot steal. If the runner is stopped between bases when the catcher retrieves the ball and the catcher throws the ball back to the pitcher near the pitcher's plate, the ball is dead and the runner must return to the last base touched. If a play is made on the runner, or if the pitcher receives the ball anywhere other than near the pitching plate, the ball is live and the runner(s) can advance.

39. SUBSTITUTIONS.

All substitutions must be reported to the plate umpire who, in turn, will report the changes to the official scorekeeper. All substitute names and numbers should be listed on the official lineup card submitted to the plate umpire at the start of the game; however, if a player is not listed on the card and is on the official roster, he can be added after the game has begun.

If a substitution is in the game without reporting, he is considered an unreported substitute. If brought to the plate umpire's attention by the offended team after the first legal or illegal pitch and before the team in violation informs the umpire, the umpire will eject him from the game. (Refer to Rule 4, Section 6 B for various situations.)

If a manager removes a substitute from the game and re-enters the same substitute later in the game, this is considered an illegal re-entry. For an illegal re-entry, the player is ejected. This would not be a forfeit. The only time a game is forfeited for a substitution violation is when a player removed by the umpire (illegal player) is back in the same game, **or if the ejection creates a situation where there are not enough players to continue the game.**

Violation of any substitution rule is handled as a protest by the offended team.

40. TIE GAMES OR GAMES CALLED WHICH ARE LESS THAN REGULATION.

When these games are rescheduled, the same procedure should be followed as stated in POE #33, PROTESTED GAME UPHELD AND RESCHEDULED.

In determining tie games after five innings (regulation game) have been played, the home team must have had the opportunity to bat and tie the score. If the home team has scored more runs than the visiting team and the game is called in the bottom of the fifth or sixth inning, the home team shall be the winner. If the visiting team has scored more runs than the home team in the sixth or seventh inning and the home team has not had the opportunity to complete its turn at bat, the game reverts back to the previous inning. If that score was tied, it would be a tie game. If the score was not tied, a winner would be declared if one team was ahead and five full innings had been played.

If a game is called before five full innings have been played (four and one-half if the home team is ahead), the game will be resumed at the point at which it was called.

41. TIE BREAKER RULE.

During each half inning of the inning used to enforce the tie breaker, the offensive team shall begin its turn at bat with the player who is scheduled to bat ninth in that respective half inning being placed at second base. (e.g., If the number five batter is to lead off, the number four batter in the batting order will be placed on second base. A substitute may be inserted for the runner.)

It is the responsibility of the umpire and scorekeeper to notify the teams involved as to what player starts at second base. If the wrong player is placed on the base and it is brought to the umpire's attention, there is no penalty. Correct the error and place the correct person on the base. This should occur whether a pitch has been thrown, or if the runner has advanced a base. If a substitute has been entered without reporting and one pitch has been thrown, the umpire should enforce the illegal substitute penalty when it is brought to his attention.

When a team is playing shorthanded and involved in the tiebreaker rule, and it is the shorthanded spot in the batting order which should start at second base, instead place on second base the player whose name precedes the absent player's name in the lineup.

In scoring, the run scored by a player starting as a runner at second base shall be charged to the defensive team and not the pitcher. Depending on the judgment of the official scorekeeper, a run scored by any other player will be charged to the pitcher's ERA.

When playing pool play in JOA and Gold fast and slow pitch tournaments, a time limit of one hour forty minutes will be in effect for each game. Should a game be tied at the conclusion of this time limit, the tie-breaker will begin with the next full inning.

Softball
Official Rules

PLAYING RULES
AND
POINTS OF EMPHASIS
INDEX

PLAYING RULES
AND POINTS OF EMPHASIS INDEX

References are by game, rule, section and article.
If a subject is explained in the Points of Emphasis, it is so noted
by a number referring to the section where it can be located.
(i.e., Appeals—POE #1)

Game Key: Specific game not indicated, refer to ALL games.
FP - Fast Pitch
SP - Slow Pitch
MP - Modified Pitch
16" - Sixteen-inch Slow Pitch

		Rule	Section	Article
ALTERED BAT				
Bat specifications		3	1	
Batter is out		7	6	B
AMERICAN DISABILITY ACT		4	2	
APPEAL PLAY (POE #1)		1		
After time out	SP	8	8	I (Effect (3)
Batting out of order		7	2	C Effect (1-4)
May not return		8	3	G
Runner		8	8	F-I
ASSISTS		11	2	B (5) (A-D)
AUTOMATIC OUT	SP	4	1	C (3)
	SP	4	1	D
BALL				
Called by umpire		7	5	A-E
Fair ball		1		

	Rule	Section	Article
BALL, Cont.			
Foul ball	1		
Intentionally thrown	8	6	K
Official	3	3	
Rotation(POE #2)			
Texture	3	3	A
Unintentionally carried (POE #18)	8	6	J
BASELINE	1		
BASE ON BALLS	1		
	8	1	C
	8	8	T (2) Note
BASE PATH	1		
Runner not out	8	9	A
Runner out	8	8	A
BASES	2	3	H
Double Base	2	3	H (1) a-e
Drawing (page 186)			
Running in legal order	8	3	A-G
BASE UMPIRE	10	3	A-B
BAT	3	1	
Hitting ball			
second time (POE #19)	7	6	I
Illegal	3	1	B
Warm-up	3	2	
With dents (POE #3)			
BATTED BALL	1		
BATTER			
Automatic out SP	4	1	C (3)
SP	4	1	D
Becomes a batter-runner	8	1	A-F
Check Swing (POE #6)			

		Rule	Section	Article
BATTER, Cont.				
Chopping down on ball	SP	1		
Enters batter's box with altered bat		7	6	B
Hindering the catcher		7	3	D
		7	6	N
Hit by pitch		7	4	F-H
	FP/MP	8	1	F
Hitting a fair ball with the bat a second time (POE #19)		7	6	I
Hitting with an illegal bat (POE #4)		7	6	C
Intentional walk		8	1	C
Not taking position in 10 seconds		7	3	B
		7	4	I
On-deck hitter		7	1	A-E
Out		7	6	A-N
Stepping across home plate while pitcher is in pitching position		7	3	D
Stepping out of batter's box (POE #6)		1		
		7	6	D
Third Strike Violation (JO Only)		7	6	L
When third out is made while at bat		7	2	E
BATTER'S BOX		1		
Dimensions		2	3	C
Drawing (page 185)				
Violation (JO Only) (POE #5)		7	3	C
BATTER-RUNNER		1		
		8	1	A-F
Accident prevents running to awarded base		4	6	D
Batter-runner is out		8	2	A-N

		Rule	Section	Article
BATTER-RUNNER, Cont.				
Going directly to first base		8	2	D
Home run does not have to run (Super SP and all Major Divisions)		8	3	I
Moving back to home		8	2	H
Overrunning first base		8	8	H
	FP/MP	8	8	T Note
Running outside three-foot line		8	2	E
BATTER'S ON-DECK CIRCLE		2	3	B
BATTING ORDER		1		
For designated player	FP/MP	4	3	
Out of order		7	2	A-E
BLOCKED BALL		1		
Offensive equipment on field		8	6	G (3)
BLOOD RULE		1		
		4	8	
BOX SCORE		11	2	A-B
BUNT (POE #8)		1		
With two strikes on batter	FP/MP	7	6	F
	SP	7	6	G
CAPS				
For players		3	6	A
For umpires		10	1	C
For Coaches		3	6	A (3)
CASTS		3	6	
CATCH		1		
Legally caught ball		1		
CATCH AND CARRY		1		
Intentionally earned out of play		8	6	K
Unintentionally carried out of play		8	6	J

		Rule	Section	Article
CATCHER'S BOX (POE #7)		1		
	FP/MP	6	7	A
	SP/16"	6	6	A
Dimensions		2	3	D
Drawing (page 185)				
CATCHER'S OBSTRUCTION		8	1	D
CHANGE OF UMPIRES		10	5	
CHARGED CONFERENCES (POE #7)				
Defensive		1		
		5	7	B
Offensive		1		
		5	7	A
Super Slow Pitch		1		
		5	7	C
CHOPPED BALL		1		
	SP	7	6	G
CLEATS		3	6	G
COACH		1		
Assists runner		8	8	E
Interferes with throw		8	8	M
		8	8	O
Removal from the game		5	7	A
		10	9	C
Two coaches		10	9	B
COACH'S BOX DIMENSIONS		2	3	E
Drawing (Page 184)				
COED RULES				
Ball		3	3	J-K
Base distances.		2	1	
Batting order		7	2	D
Defensive positioning.		4	1	C (5)

		Rule	Section	Article
COED RULES, Cont.				
Extra player (EP)		4	1	C (6)
		4	4	E
Male base on balls		8	1	C (3)
Outfield distance		2	1	
Pitching distance		2	1	
Shoes		3	6	G
Starting Game		4	1	C (5) & (6)
Uniforms		3	6	
Use of the wrong ball		3	3	J-K Effect
CONDITION OF FIELD		5	2	
COURTESY RUNNER		1		
Senior 55-Over division	SP	8	10	A
CRASH (RUNNER) **(POE #12)**		8	8	Q
CROW HOP	FP	1		
DEAD BALL		1		
Intentionally carrying into dead ball area (POE #21)		8	6	K
DEFENSIVE TEAM		1		
Defensive player distracts batter	FP/MP	6	5	B
	SP/16"	6	4	B
Throwing glove at ball		8	6	F
DEFINITIONS		1		
DELAYED DEAD BALL (POE #11)				
Catcher obstruction		8	1	D
Detached equipment hitting ball		8	6	F
Illegal pitch	FP/MP	6	1-8	
	SP/16"	6	1-7	

		Rule	Section	Article
DELAYED DEAD BALL, Cont.				
Obstruction		8	6	B
Plate umpire interference		8	7	F
Signal		10	7	K
DESIGNATED PLAYER (DP) (POE #13)	FP	4	3	A-G
Penalty for illegal DP		4	3	G Effect
Scoring		11	2	A (1)
DETACHED EQUIPMENT		8	6	F
DIAMOND DIMENSIONS		2	1	
Official dimensions of softball field (page 184)				
DISABLED PLAYER (ADA)		4	2	
DISLODGED BASE		1		
Following a base		8	3	C
Not out if off dislodged base		8	9	N
Runner attempts to continue		8	5	C
DISQUALIFIED PLAYER		1		
Home Run Rule		5	8	F, G, H
DOUBLE BASE		2	3	H
Batter-runner touching white portion during play		8	2	M
DOUBLE, GROUND RULE		8	6	H,I
DOUBLE PLAY		1		
DROPPED BALL DURING WINDUP	FP/MP	6	11	
	SP	6	9	D
	16"	6	9	C
DROPPED THIRD STRIKE	FP	8	1	B

	Rule	Section	Article
DUGOUT	1		
Conduct (POE #14)	5	12	
EJECTION FROM GAME	5	4	G-H
Altered bat	7	6	B
Crash	8	8	Q
Second offense	10	9	C
	5	7	A
Violation of the rules	10	1	J (3)
EQUIPMENT	3	1-7	
Left on field (POE #15)			
ERROR	11	2	B (6) A-E
EXTRA PLAYER (EP) (POE#16) SP	4	4	A-F
Minimum number of players	4	1	C (4), (6)
Penalty	4	4	A
	4	5	A
Scoring	11	2	A (2)
Two (Senior SP)	4	4	F
FAIR BALL	1		
FAIR TERRITORY	1		
FAKE TAG (POE #17)	1		
FIELDER	1		
FITNESS OF GROUND	5	2	
FLY BALL	1		
Carried into dead ball area	8	6	J
FORCE OUT	1		
	8	8	G

		Rule	Section	Article
FOREIGN SUBSTANCE ON PITCHING HAND	FP/MP	6	6	
	SP/16"	6	5	
FORFEITED GAME		5	4	A-I
Score of		5	6	C
Records		11	9	
FOUL BALL		1		
FOUL TIP		1		
		7	4	C
GAME CALLED		5	3	C
GLOVES		3	4	
Illegal glove usage		8	9	O
Softball glove specifications		3	4	
GROUND RULES		2	2	
Discussion with managers		10	1	E
GROUND RULE DOUBLE		8	6	H,I
HEADBANDS		3	6	A (2)
HEADWEAR		3	6	A
Mixed headwear		3	6	A (2)
HEIGHT OF PITCH	SP	6	3	H
	16"	6	3	D
HELMET		1		
Cracked, broken, altered		3	5	D (1)
Usage		3	5	D
HESITATION PITCH	16"	6	3	F
HIT BATSMAN		7	4	F-H
		7	6	A
	FP	8	1	F

		Rule	Section	Article
HOME PLATE		2	3	G
Drawing (Page 186)				
HOME RUN		8	6	H
Home Run Rule	SP	5	8	
Running Bases (Super & Men's Major SP)(POE #20)		8	3	1 Exception
HOME TEAM		1		
ILLEGAL BAT		1		
Legal Bat		3	1	
ILLEGALLY BATTED BALL		1		
		8	7	B
ILLEGAL BATTER		1		
		4	3	G
ILLEGALLY CAUGHT BALL				
Detached equipment		8	6	F
Illegal glove		8	9	O
ILLEGAL PITCH	FP/MP	6	1-8	Effect
	SP/16"	6	1-7	Effect
ILLEGAL PITCHER		1		
Excessive speed	SP	6	3	G
Motion before stepping on plate	SP	6	1	D
Removed from position		4	6	B (3)
ILLEGAL RE-ENTRY		1		
ILLEGAL RUNNER		1		
		4	6	B1(e)
ILLEGAL SUBSTITUTE		1		
Offense		4	6	B (1)
Defense		4	6	B (2)

		Rule	Section	Article
INCOMPLETE GAME		5	3	D,F
INELIGIBLE PLAYER		1		
INFIELD		1		
INFIELD FLY		1		
		8	2	I
IN FLIGHT		1		
IN JEOPARDY		1		
INJURED RUNNER		4	1	D
		4	8	
INNINGS		1		
Regulation games		5	3	
INSULTING REMARKS TOWARD PLAYERS OR UMPIRES		10	9	A
INTENTIONALLY DROPPED FLY BALL (POE #22)		8	2	J
INTENTIONAL WALK (POE #23 & 24)	SP 8	1	C(2)	
INTERFERENCE (POE #25)		1		
Aiding a runner		8	8	E
At home plate		8	8	M
Ball hitting umpire		8	1	E
By base coach		8	8	E,M,O
By batter		7	3	D
		7	6	N
By on-deck batter		7	1	E
By plate umpire	FP/MP	8	7	F
By runner		8	8	J,K,L,P,Q

		Rule	Section	Article
INTERFERENCE, Cont.				
Catcher with batter on attempted squeeze play	FP/MP	6	5	C
Crash by runner (POE #12)		8	8	Q
Offensive equipment on field		8	6	G (3)
Runners return		8	7	C
		8	8	J-Q Effect
Spectator		8	2	N
		8	6	L
While fielding foul ball		7	6	H
With a bat		7	6	I
JEWELRY		3	6	F
Medical Alert Bracelets/ Necklaces		3	6	F Note
JUNIOR OLYMPIC PLAYER		1		
LEAPING	FP	1		
LEAVE GAME (RE-ENTRY)		4	5	
Substitutes		4	6	
LEGAL DELIVERY OR PITCH	FP/MP	6	3	A-M
	SP	6	3	A-K
	16"	6	3	A-H
LEGALLY CAUGHT BALL (CATCH)		1		
LEGAL TOUCH		1		
LINE DRIVE		1		
LOOK BACK RULE (POE #26)		8	8	T
LOSS, CREDITED TO PITCHER		11	6	

		Rule	Section	Article
MASKS AND THROAT PROTECTORS		3	5	
Umpires		10	1	C
Catchers	FP	3	5	C Note
Face Masks		3	5	E
MAXIMUM/MINIMUM ARC	SP	6	3	H
	16"	6	3	D
MEDIA COVERAGE (POE #27)				
MITTS		3	4	
Illegal mitt penalty		8	9	O
MODIFIED PITCHING RULES	MP	6	1-11	
MODIFIED PITCHING RULES, Cont.				
Ball	MP	3	3	J
Class A and 10-man delivery	MP	6	3	F(2-3) H(2)
Major delivery	MP	6	3	F(1) H(1)
MULTI-COLORED GLOVES	FP	3	4	
NO PITCH	FP/MP	6	10	A-E
	SP	6	9	A-E
	16"	6	9	A-C
NUMBERS, UNIFORM		3	6	D
OBSTRUCTION (POE #28)		1		
		8	6	B
Catcher obstruction		8	1	D
OFFENSIVE TEAM		1		
OFFICIAL BALL - 11", 12", 16"		3	3	

		Rule	Section	Article
OFFICIAL SCOREKEEPER		11	1	
ON-DECK BATTER		1		
		7	1	A-E
Warm-up bats		3	2	
ON-DECK CIRCLE DIMENSIONS		2	3	B
Drawing (page 186)				
OUTFIELD		1		
OVERRUN FIRST BASE (POE #29)		8	8	H
OVERSLIDE		1		
Runner is out		8	8	H
OVERTHROW (POE #30)		1		
		8	6	G
From pitching plate	FP/MP	8	6	C
PASSED BALL		1		
PICK OFF	16"	6	3	F(4) a-e
PINE TAR		3	1	J
PITCH				
Delivered with catcher out of catcher's box	FP/MP	6	5	A
	SP/16"	6	4	A
Height of pitch	SP	6	3	H
	16"	6	3	D
Illegal	FP/MP	6	1-8	Effect
	SP/16"	6	1-7	Effect
No pitch declared	FP/MP	6	10	A-E
	SP	6	9	A-E
	16"	6	9	A-C
Quick return pitch	FP/MP	6	10	B
	SP/16"	6	7	

		Rule	**Section**	**Article**
PITCH, Cont.				
Returned by catcher	FP/MP	6	7	B
	SP/16"	6	6	B
Slips from pitcher's hand	FP/MP	6	11	
	SP	6	9	D
	16"	6	9	B
Warm-up pitches allowed	FP/MP	6	9	
	SP/16"	6	8	
PITCH BEGINS **(POE #31 - FP)**	FP/MP	6	2	
	SP/16"	6	2	
PITCHER				
Batting glove on pitching hand	FP/MP	6	6	
	SP/16"	6	5	
Credited with loss		11	6	
Credited with win		11	5	A-B
Defensive conference		1		
		5	7	B
Deliberately dropped or rolled ball	FP/MP	6	3	L
Fails to pitch ball within allotted time	FP/MP	6	3	M
	SP	6	3	
	16"	6	3	G
Foreign substance on ball	FP/MP	6	6	
	SP/16"	6	6	
Hesitation throws	16"	6	3	F
Legal delivery	FP/MP	6	3	A-M
	SP	6	3	A-K
	16"	6	3	A-G
Pick-off attempts	16"	6	3	F (4) a-e
Playing runners back to base from eight-foot circle	FP/MP	8	8	T

		Rule	Section	Article
PITCHER, Cont.				
Position of feet	FP	6	1	A,C
	MP	6	1	A
Step during delivery	FP	6	3	G
	MP	6	3	J
Removal after conference with manager		1		
		5	7	B
Starting pitcher		1		
Re-enter		4	5	C
Tape on finger	FP/MP	6	6	
	SP/16"	6	5	
Penalty for illegal pitch		7	5	B
Uniform (POE #32)				
Warm-up pitches allowed between innings	FP/MP	6	9	
	SP/16"	6	8	
PITCHER'S PLATE		2	3	F
Contact at delivery	FP	6	3	G,H
	MP	6	3	J,K
	SP	6	3	E
	16"	6	3	A
Drawing (page 186)				
Eight-foot circle		2	3	F
Pitcher throws while in contact with	FP/MP	6	8	
	16"	6	3	F (4) a
PITCHER'S SIGNALS	FP/MP	6	1	B
PITCHING DISTANCES		2	1	
PITCHING POSITION	FP/MP	6	1	A-E
	SP	6	1	A-C
	16"	6	1	A-E
PIVOT FOOT		1		

	Rule	Section	Article
PLATE UMPIRE	10	2	A-F
PLAY BALL	1		
Fail to resume play in two minutes	5	4	C,D
PLAY MADE BY UNANNOUNCED SUBSTITUTE	4	6	A,B
PLAYERS	4	1	A-D
Disabled (ADA Rule)	4	2	
Minimum number to play	4	1	C,D
Officially entering the game	4	6	A,B
Positions	4	1	C (1-7)
Removed from the game	4	6	C
Short-handed rule	4	1	D
PLAYING FIELD	2	1-3	
Drawing (page 187)			
Fitness for play	5	2	
PROSTHESIS USAGE	3	6	E
PROTESTS (POE #33)	9	1-7	
Correcting errors	9	2	A
Decisions	9	7	A-C
Examples	9	1	
Information needed	9	6	
Notification of intent	9	4	A-B
Time limit	9	5	
Types	9	2	A-C
QUICK RETURN PITCH	1		
FP/MP	6	10	B
SP/16"	6	7	
RE-ENTER GAME	4	5	
RE-ENTRY, PENALTY FOR ILLEGAL	4	5	A-C

		Rule	Section	Article
REFUSING TO PLAY		5	4	B-D
REGULATION GAME		5	3	
REMOVAL FROM GAME		5	4	G,H
Batter using altered bat		7	6	B
Manager or coach		5	7	A
Re-entry		4	5	A
Substitute not announced		4	6	
Second offense		10	9	C
Violation of rules		10	1	J (3)
RESIN	FP/MP	6	6	
	SP/16"	6	5	
RETURN OF PITCH **TO PITCHER**	FP/MP	6	7	B
	SP/16"	6	6	B
REVERSAL OF **UMPIRE'S DECISION**		10	6	B
ROSTERS **(MALE AND FEMALE)**		4	1	B
RUN AHEAD RULE		5	9	
RUNNER		1		
Abandons base		8	8	U
Assisted by anyone		8	8	E
Award of bases on overthrow of ball				
out of play		8	3	I
correcting errors on awards		8	6	G(4)
		9	2	A
		8	6	C Effect
		8	6	G
Base stealing		8	4	A
	SP	8	7	G

	Rule	Section	Article
RUNNER, Cont.			
Bases touched in legal order	8	3	
Coach draws throw at home	8	8	M
Comes into contact with fielder attemptiing to field ball	8	8	J
Comes in contact with fielder not entitled to field ball	8	9	C
Courtesy runner (Seniors)	8	10	A
Deliberate contact with a fielder with the ball	8	8	Q
Enters team area	8	8	U
Entitled to advance with liability to be put out	8	4	A-H
Entitled to advance without liability to be put out	8	6	A-K
Fails to keep contact with base until pitched ball reaches home plate SP	8	8	R
Fails to keep contact with base until ball leaves the pitcher's hand FP	8	8	S
Fails to return to base or proceed to next base when ball is in the eight-foot circle FP	8	8	T 1-2
Hit by batted ball (POE #35)	8	9	D-F
Homerun does not have to run (Super & all Major Men's Divisions)	8	3	I
Illegal pitch FP/MP	8	6	E
Illegal runner	4	6	B1 (e)
Intentionally kicking ball	8	8	L

		Rule	Section	Article
RUNNER, Cont.				
Interferes with play after being declared out		8	8	P
Interferes with the play before being declared out		8	8	J
Leaving base after returning	FP	8	8	T (2)
Leaving base on an appeal		8	8	F-I Effect
Leaving base too soon		8	3	H
		8	9	L
Leading off	SP	8	7	G (Effect)
	FP	8	8	S
	16"	8	5	D
Misses home plate		8	8	I
Must return to his base		8	7	A-H
Not out		8	9	A-O
Obstructed		8	6	B
Offensive team collecting to confuse the defense		8	8	N
Out		8	8	A-X
Overruns first base and attempts to go to second		8	8	H
Passes another runner		8	8	D
Running the bases in reverse order		8	3	D
Running out of baseline		8	8	A
Running start		8	8	V
Struck by fair ball while off base		8	8	K
Struck by fair ball while on base		8	9	M
Two occupying a base at the same time		8	3	E
RUNS BATTED IN		11	4	A-G
RUNS NOT SCORED		5	5	B
		8	3	F
Force out		5	5	B (1)

		Rule	Section	Article
RUNS SCORED (POE #34)		5	5	A
SACRIFICE FLY		1		
SENIOR SLOW PITCH RULES				
Courtesy runner	SP	8	10	A
Courtesy runner out		8	8	X
Second courtesy runner		8	10	A
Double first base	SP	2	3	H (2)
Double home plate	SP	2	3	G (1)
		8	10	B
Extra player	SP	4	4	F
No return line	SP	8	10	C
SCOREKEEPER'S SUMMARY		11	7	A-T
SCORING		11	1-10	
Base hit		11	3	A-D
Excessive home runs		11	2	B (4) b
Forfeited game records		11	9	
Runs		5	5	
Tie-breaker		11	10	
SHOES (POE #36)		3	6	G
SHORT-HANDED TEAMS (POE #37)		4	1	D
Forfeit		5	4	J
In tie breaker		5	10	A
Starting less than ten	SP	4	1	C (3)
SINGLE UMPIRE		10	4	
SIXTEEN-INCH SLOW PITCH RULES				
Ball		3	3	
Base distance		2	1	

		Rule	Section	Article
SIXTEEN-INCH SLOW PITCH RULES, Cont.				
Foul tip		7	4	C
Lead off		8	7	G Exception
		8	5	D
Pick off		6	3	F (4) c
Pitching		6	1-9	
Pitching distance		2	1	
Pitching hesitation		6	3	F (1-4)
Outfield distance		2	1	
SOFTBALL - 11", 12", & 16"		3	3	
SPECTATORS, ABUSIVE LANGUAGE		10	9	A
Attack umpire		5	4	A
SPEED OF PITCH	SP	6	3	G
	16"	6	3	C
SPIKES		3	6	G
Youth, Seniors, & Coed		3	6	G
STARTING LINEUP		4	1	
Number of players		4	1	
Positions		4	1	C
Re-enter		4	5	
STARTING PITCHER		1		
STEALING (POE #38)		1		
	SP	8	7	G
Baserunner out		8	8	S
Leaving bases after returning	FP/MP	8	8	T
Scoring	FP	11	8	
Super & Men's Major only	SP	8	4	G
When ball leaves pitcher's hand	FP/MP	8	4	A

		Rule	Section	Article
STEP TAKEN BY				
A PITCHER	FP	6	3	G
	MP	6	3	J
	SP	6	3	E
	16"	6	3	A
STEPPING OUT OF				
BATTER'S BOX		7	6	D
		7	3	C
STRIKE		7	4	A-J
Ball hitting batter				
on third strike		7	4	F-G
Dropped third strike		8	1	B
STRIKE ZONE	FP	1		
	SP	1		
SUBSTITUTE (POE #39)		1		
Courtesy runner (Seniors)		8	10	A (1-5)
No substitute available		5	4	H
		4	1	D
Notify umpire		4	6	A
Officially in game		4	6	B 1-2
Re-enter		4	5	
Unannounced (illegal)		4	6	B 1-2
SUBSTITUTE RUNNER				
Automatic out		4	1	D 3
Injury to runner		4	6	D
SUPER SLOW PITCH RULES				
Ball		2	3	L
Base distance		2	1	
Conferences		5	7	C
Home run rule		5	8	A
Language		10	6	A
Outfield distance		2	1	
Pitching distance		2	1	

		Rule	Section	Article
SUPER SLOW PITCH RULES, Cont.				
Run ahead		5	9	A (4)
Stealing		1		
		8	4	G
		8	7	G
Touching bases		8	3	I
SUSPENSION OF PLAY		5	4	D
		10	8	A-I
TAPE ON PITCHING HAND	FP/MP	6	6	
	SP/16"	6	5	
TEAM		4	1	
Home team		5	1	
Refusing to play		5	4	B-D
To continue playing		4	1	A
Delay or hasten game		5	4	E
To start a game		4	1	A
TEN-UNDER RULES				
Ball		3	3	I, K
Stealing		8	4	H
Third strike out and ball dead		8	1	B
THIRD STRIKE RULE (POE #36)	FP/MP	8	1	B
		7	6	L
	SP	7	6	J
	SP	7	4	C
THREE-FOOT LINE DIMENSIONS		2	3	A
Drawing (Page 184)				
THROAT PROTECTORS (MASKS)		3	5	A-C
Umpires		10	1	C

		Rule	Section	Article
THROWING TO A BASE WHILE FOOT IS IN CONTACT WITH PITCHER'S PLATE	FP/MP	6	8	
	16"	6	3	F (4) a
THROWING GLOVE AT BALL		8	6	F
TIE GAMES (POE #40)		5	3	B, E, F
Regulation tie		5	3	E
Tie breaker (POE #38)		5	10	
TIME		1		
By umpire		10	8	A-I
Player, manager, coach	FP/MP	6	10	E
	SP	6	9	E
	16"	6	9	E
TIME LIMIT RULE		5	10	
TRAPPED CATCH		8	2	J
		1		
TRIPLE PLAY		1		
TURN AT BAT		1		
UMPIRES		10	1-9	
Equipment/uniform		10	1	C
Hit by thrown ball		10	8	E
Interference		8	1	E
		10	8	D
Interference (plate umpire)	FP	8	7	F
Judgement		10	6	
Signals		10	7	A-R
Reversal of decision		10	6	B
UNIFORMS				
For players		3	6	

		Rule	Section	Article
UNIFORMS, Cont.				
Mixed long/short pants	SP	3	6	B
For umpires		10	1	C
Numbers on uniform		3	6	D
VIOLATIONS		10	9	A-C
WALK (BASE ON BALLS)		1		
		8	1	C
		8	8	T (2) Note
WARM-UP BATS		3	2	
WARM-UP PITCHES				
FOR A RELIEF PITCHER	FP/MP	6	9	
	SP/16"	6	8	
		7	5	E
WILD PITCH		1		
Goes out of play	FP/MP	8	6	C
WIN CREDITED TO PITCHER		11	5	A-B
WINDUP	FP/MP	6	3	M
	SP	6	3	A-K
	16"	6	3	A-H
WINNING TEAM		5	6	
WRISTBANDS ON				
PITCHER	FP/MP	6	6	
	SP/16"	6	5	
YOUTH DIFFERENCES				
Batter's box violation		7	3	C
Catchers		3	5	C
Warm-up		3	5	C Note

	Rule	Section	Article
YOUTH DIFFERENCES, Cont.			
Helmets	3	5	D (1)
On-deck batters	3	5	D (1)
Coaching	3	5	D (1)
Metal spikes	3	6	G
Field dimensions	2	1	
Third Strike Violation	7	6	L
Strike called by umpire	7	4	J
(Also see 10-Under rules)			

Softball
Official Rules

APPENDIX

DIAGRAM 1
SOFTBALL DIAMOND

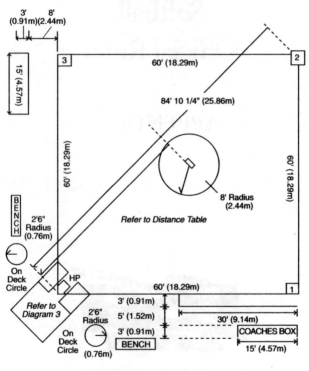

*For base distances, pitching distances, and
fence distances, see Rule 2, Section 1.*

DIAGRAM 2
HOME PLATE TO SECOND BASE

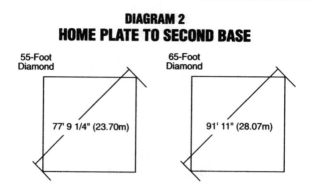

55-Foot
Diamond

77' 9 1/4" (23.70m)

65-Foot
Diamond

91' 11" (28.07m)

DIAGRAM 3
HOME PLATE DETAILS AND CATCHER'S BOX

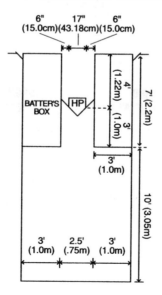

6"
(15.0cm)

17"
(43.18cm)

6"
(15.0cm)

BATTER'S
BOX

HP

4'
(1.22m)

3'
(1.0m)

7' (2.2m)

3'
(1.0m)

10' (3.05m)

3'
(1.0m)

2.5'
(.75m)

3'
(1.0m)

DIAGRAM 4
PITCHER'S PLATE

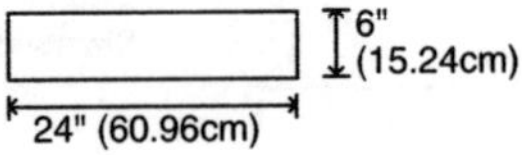

6"
(15.24cm)

24" (60.96cm)

DIAGRAM 5
ON DECK CIRCLE

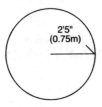

2'5"
(0.75m)

DIAGRAM 6
HOME PLATE

DIAGRAM 7
BASE

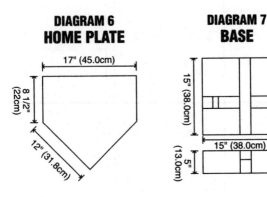

17" (45.0cm)

8 1/2"
(22cm)

12" (31.8cm)

15" (38.0cm)

15" (38.0cm)

5"
(13.0cm)

DIAGRAM 8
INFIELD, OUTFIELD, AND BACKSTOP

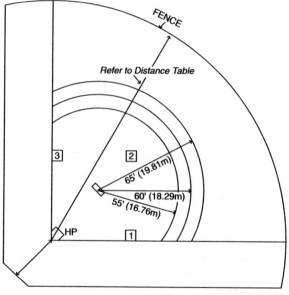

FENCE

Refer to Distance Table

3

2

65' (19.81m)

60' (18.29m)

55' (16.76m)

HP

1

Backstop should be a minimum of 25' (7.62m) or a maximum of 30' (9.14m) from home plate.

Skinned Infields: A 55' (16.76m) and 60' (18.29m) radius may be used with the front center of the 46'(14.02m) pitcher's plate as the center point of the arc. The 60' (18.29m) is recommended for 60' bases. For 65' bases, a 65' (19.81m radius is recommended.

*ASA Playing Rules will be in effect in all college softball
with these modifications.*

NAIA MODIFICATIONS

The Amateur Softball Association (ASA) rules shall be followed by all NAIA affiliate programs for the 1998 season, with the following changes or modifications:

1. PITCHING DISTANCE.
(Rule 2, Section 3) The pitching distance will be 43 feet.

2. SKINNED INFIELDS.
All infields must be skinned for conference/sectional, regional and national championship play.

3. OUTFIELD FENCE DISTANCE.
Outfield fence distance shall be a minimum of 200 feet and a maximum of 225 feet for all NAIA regional and national championship competition.

4. A five-inning eight run rule shall be used.

5. There shall be no time limit or tie breaker rule used during NAIA postseason play. It may be used during the regular season.

NCAA MODIFICATIONS

The NCAA has their own official rule book.

NJCAA FAST PITCH SOFTBALL RULES

SECTION 5. RULES AND PROCEDURES

  a. Current ASA Rules will be used with the following exceptions:

    1. Catchers are required to wear helmets.

    2. The pitching distance shall be 43 feet.

    3. No international tie breaking rule for tournament play.

    4. The eight run rule shall be used in tournament play.

  b. The tournament shall be conducted as a double elimination fast pitch tournament.

  c. All region/district hosts will use and be furnished the official tournament ball in all post-season play with the exception of regions within a district, which will receive balls only for a district tournament.

  d. The official tournament ball is the Dudley WT12YFP.

NJCAA SLOW PITCH SOFTBALL RULES

SECTION 5. RULES AND PROCEDURES

  a. Current ASA rules will be used.

  b. ASA official 11-inch softballs (co-efficient of .47) shall be used.

  c. The 12-run rule will be in effect after the 5th inning except in the championship game(s).

  d. Helmets and masks for catchers are recommended for the National Invitational Softball Tournaments.

  e. Steel cleats may not be worn by participating players.

AMATEUR SOFTBALL ASSOCIATION
•
USA SOFTBALL

The Amateur Softball Association (ASA) has many important responsibilities as the national governing body of softball in the United States including regulating competition to insure fairness and equal opportunity to the millions of players who annually play the sport.

When the ASA entered the softball picture in 1933, the sport was in a state of confusion with no unified set of playing rules and no national governing body to provide guidance and stability. The ASA changed all that by adopting the sport's first universally accepted rules of play and organizing consistent and fair competition across the nation.

From this beginning, the ASA has become one of the nation's largest and fastest growing sports organizations and now sanctions competition in every state through a network of 101 state and metro associations. The ASA has grown from a few hundred teams in the early days to over 260,000 teams today representing a membership of more than four million.

The ASA provides the sport with leadership through an extensive number of programs including the following:

- **USA Softball Olympic and National Teams**
  Working in conjunction with the United States Olympic Committee (USOC), the ASA is responsible for the selection and preparation of the USA softball

teams that represent the nation in international competition including World Championships, the Pan American Games and the Olympics. Recognized through the Amateur Sports Act of 1978, the ASA is the only softball organization to have ever been designated as the official national governing body (NGB) for the sport.

- **Junior Olympic Youth Program**
  The ASA Junior Olympic Youth Program is among the nation's largest youth sports programs with over 78,000 teams and 1 million players and 300,000 coaches involved annually. It is the single fastest growing program in the ASA and has increased in membership enrollment every year for over two decades.

- **Umpire Program**
  The ASA umpire program is the largest officiating organization in the nation with 56,000 officials actively involved each year. ASA officials are nationally recognized as the best trained and proficient in the sport and are involved in competition starting with league play, city, state and national championships and ultimately world championship competition. All of the USA officials used in the 1996 Olympic Games were members of the ASA.

- **Coaches' Education and Volunteer Improvement Program**
  Along with the title of national governing body comes the responsibility of educating and training the coaches and athletes who participate. The ASA responds with an extensive offering of National Coaching Schools each year which are purposed to train those who are teaching the sport. Also included is the Volunteer Improvement Program (VIP), which allows coaches to receive instructional support and direction as they progress through their coaching careers.

- **National Softball Hall of Fame**
  The National Softball Hall of Fame is the final destination for any player, coach or umpire who aspires to greatness in the sport. With less than 200 inductees, the National Softball Hall of Fame is reputed to be among the hardest sports halls in the nation in which to gain membership. The National Softball Hall of Fame Museum in Oklahoma City pays tribute to the legacy of those who have made major impacts on the sport's development.

- **National Championships**
  Annually the ASA conducts over 60 National Championships across the nation in each of its major disciplines in the sport-slow, fast, and modified pitch. Since each competitor must earn its berth into an ASA national through a network of qualifying tournaments conducted throughout the season, the champion goes home as the unchallenged best team in the nation in its division each year. The economic impact on local communities across America hosting these events is estimated collectively at over $25 million.

- **State and Local League and Tournament Competition**
  Thousands of tournaments and local league games are conducted each year by the 101 state and metro associations which make up the ASA. Over four million players participate in local ASA programs each year.

NOTES

NOTES

NOTES

NOTES

NOTES